Designer's Dictionary

by

Bruce T. Barber

Director of Advertising

Published by

THE UPSON COMPANY

Lockport, New York 14094

Printed in the United States

1974

The Designer's Dictionary is the culmination of two years of research and development. It is our greatest undertaking to date.

In 1965, when I joined The Upson Company, I was impressed with the quality of Upson Board and its potential uses. To be realistic, viewing a piece of Upson Board is not the most exciting experience I've ever had, however, the excitement is the transformation of that very fine piece of material into many beautiful, imaginative things.

In 1966 we started a series of idea books for "the trade". The first was called, "How to be the Cut-Up with Upson and Get the Squarest Deal Around". This was followed by "The Second Annual Cut-Up Book". In 1970 we produced "How to Build a Better World and Show What Stuff We're Made Of", based on international themes. In '72 our promotion was a set of 4 idea posters, entitled, "The Upson Alphabet Boards". Regretfully, all of these are now out of print.

The Designer's Dictionary started with a few odd file folders of clippings and sketches. These developed into two full file drawers and from there to 30 ring binders that started to crystalize the sections and promotions. In Spring of 1973 we were ready to bring the book into physical form and luckily, we met Bob Eby of Eby Associates of Niagara Falls, Ontario, who represented the Illustrator-Designer, Tony Kew.

The book had its format, fleshed out with two years of research, clippings, sketches and countless trips to the library. Now I had the person who could really bring the ideas into creative form, and this, Tony has done. Not every sketch in the book is his work, but 90% of them are, along with the front and back covers.

As our sections developed and expanded, we looked for interesting sources of materials and services to compliment our ideas. It is important to know, I think, that the Upson Company has not charged any of these firms for mentioning their products in our book. In most cases *we* contacted them, so we really do not have a vested interest in their appearance here. We have learned from past experience that the sources of supply have been a valuable part of our books efforts and we thank all of them for their cooperation.

SOME NOTES ABOUT THESE SUPPLIERS — It is important to remember that we have worked with manufacturers and distributors on a national level. All suppliers listed are wholesalers. In some cases we have tried to give you indications of costs. All of these suppliers have minimum purchases and require credit ratings. Only inquiries on *Business Stationary* will be honored and it will be helpful if you mention the Designer's Dictionary, so that they have an idea of the source of interest.

The retail display and exhibit industry is an exciting business and the core of the excitement is the creativity that it generates. We hope that this book stimulates more creativity and cooperation between designer and supplier. In our view the entire industry prospers when everyone cooperates.

Your comments and ideas for future books are always welcome and believe it or not, our next book is well underway, but for now, we hope you enjoy "The Designer's Dictionary".

BRUCE T. BARBER
Director of Advertising
THE UPSON COMPANY

Contents

ACES

Gerstenberg

Garganico

VonRichthofen

Wolff

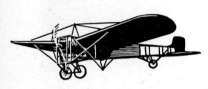

The legendary Rittmeister Manfred Freiherr Von Richthofen inspired this section called, "ACES". Few heroic exploits match the daring of the swashbuckling Von Richthofen and the other World War I fighter pilots. In his red Fokker Triplane he was dubbed the "Red Baron" and the suggested men's shop idea utilizes the symbols and materials of the period.

The central display piece is a reproduction of a British Sopwith Camel (It could be a Fokker, of course) produced in flat and three dimensional form with ¼" pebbled Upson board. Use a single 4 x 8 panel. Two panels could be used if a larger plane is desired. The main form can be made using a Cutawl and an additional authentic touch can be achieved by adding actual guy wires between the wings.

Other modifications could be the use of corrugated galvanized steel or aluminum sheets to simulate an old plane hangar. Sand textured walls can be achieved by "flats" of Upson panels and covered in sand textured paints, available at most hardware stores. Sand bags, propellers, engines and other flying paraphernalia can also be added.

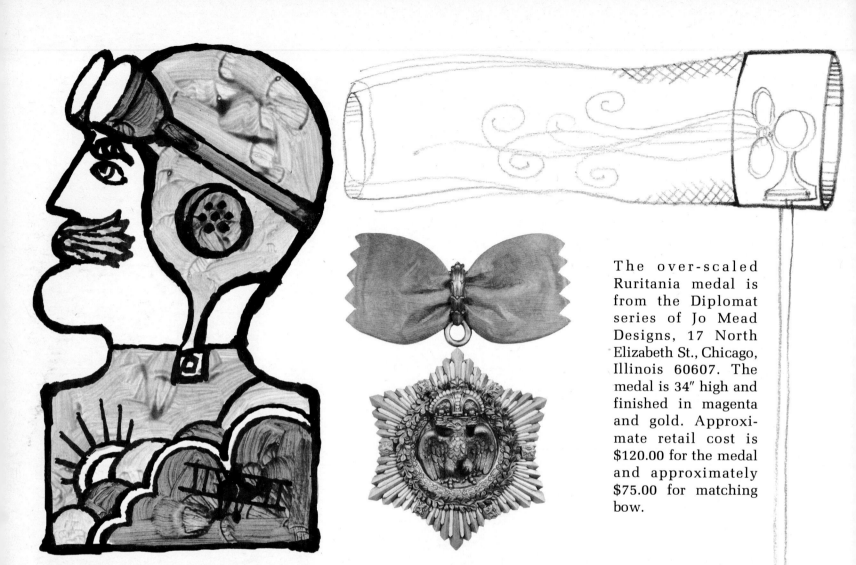

The over-scaled Ruritania medal is from the Diplomat series of Jo Mead Designs, 17 North Elizabeth St., Chicago, Illinois 60607. The medal is 34″ high and finished in magenta and gold. Approximate retail cost is $120.00 for the medal and approximately $75.00 for matching bow.

Von Richthofen's

Echelon Publishing Company, 5001 W. 78th St., Minneapolis, Minnesota 55437, produces a series of full color reproductions of many of the great World War I planes. They are 16″ x 20″ and when framed or matted, they will contribute to the atmosphere of your shop.

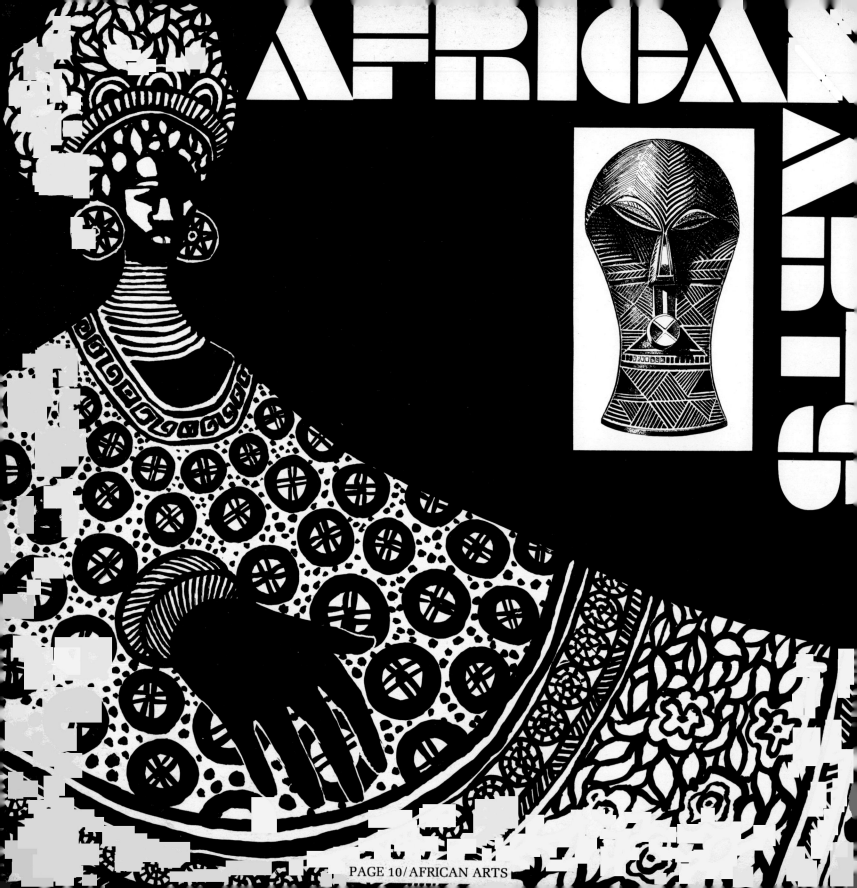

Traditional art reaches far back into the history of Africa and the pure power of the motifs indicate how truly advanced the artists were in terms of abstract design and patterns. In the case of some decorations these artisans were amazingly sophisticated in scope. Most critics agree that Picasso, Braque and many other impressionists and expressionists were influenced by the African designs on masks, tribal shields, etc.

This section, African Arts, started with a fascination with the native walls of the N'debele people in the Republic of South Africa. These people live within a hundred miles of Johannesburg, in villages set in the blazing sun of the South African landscape. The women of the village take great pride in keeping their homes esthetically pleasing for their menfolk. After the man has built a house for his bride, she takes complete charge of the ornamentation. These designs are masterpieces of simplicity with their broad, bold strokes and bright, rich colors.

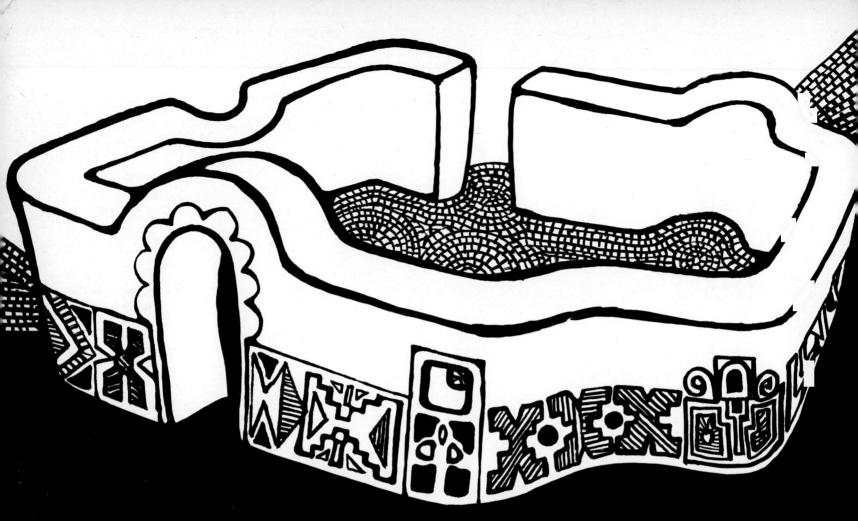

The key piece centers around a boutique idea using the thick, beautifully designed walls as its perimeter. You will be able to erect racks, shelving, open tables, etc. to sell authentic African clothing, fabrics, crafts, and other merchandise.

The travel advisors at the South African Tourist Corporation (Rockefeller Center, 610 Fifth Ave., New York 10020) have been most generous in furnishing some outstanding examples of these beautiful decorative designs.

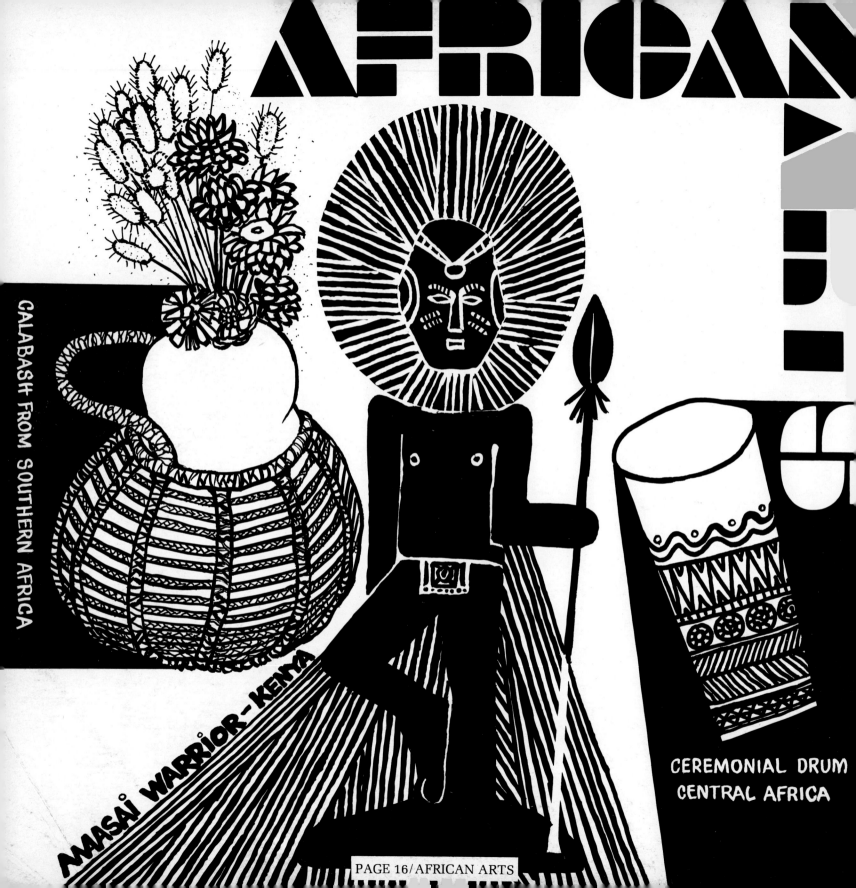

AFRICAN

ART

GALABASH FROM SOUTHERN AFRICA

MAASAI WARRIOR - KENYA

CEREMONIAL DRUM
CENTRAL AFRICA

The Kano northern Nigerian hut could make a stunning shop within a shop, with its richly decorated dimensional walls constructed by cutting different thicknesses of Upson board and painting them a rich earthen brown.

ANAGA MASK
EST AFRICA.

ZULU TRIBESMAN SOUTHERN AFRICA

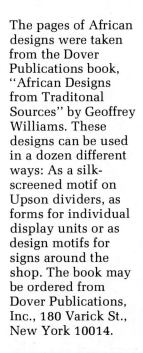
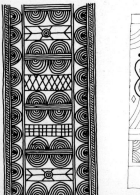
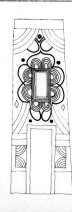

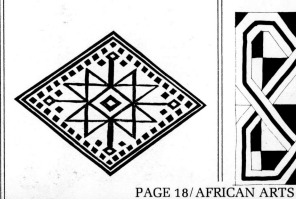

The pages of African designs were taken from the Dover Publications book, "African Designs from Traditonal Sources" by Geoffrey Williams. These designs can be used in a dozen different ways: As a silk-screened motif on Upson dividers, as forms for individual display units or as design motifs for signs around the shop. The book may be ordered from Dover Publications, Inc., 180 Varick St., New York 10014.

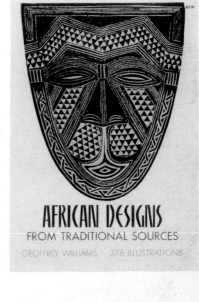

AFRICAN DESIGNS
FROM TRADITIONAL SOURCES
GEOFFREY WILLIAMS   378 ILLUSTRATIONS

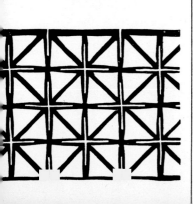

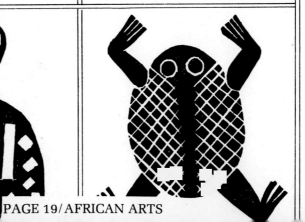

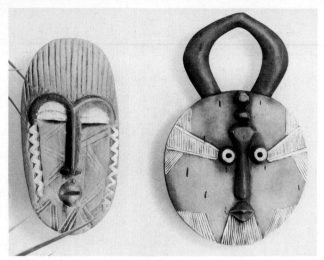

Many firms import African art. One in particular produces an exciting collection of African sculpture reproductions. They range from bronze-finished Benin carved plaques, to Basonage ancestor masks, Baule Buffalo masks, ancestral totems and many others. The supplier is Cosco Collections, 2525 State St., Columbus, Indiana 47201.

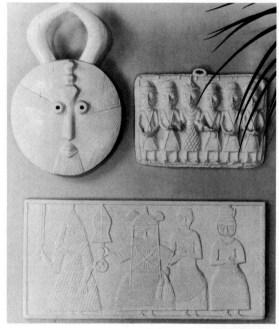

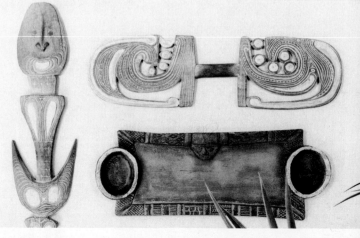

ALASKA

It's often difficult to comprehend that our forty-ninth state is twice as big as Texas and as far west as Hawaii. Alaska offers unlimited promotional possibilities. The old capital of Sitka was Russian with a Ukrainian heritage. It began to be westernized when the gold rush opened the land to prospectors and adventurers. Design possibilities are virtually unlimited. Your in-store promotion could center around the old Klondike days, the gold rush or the gay nineties. They could include the crafts and design motifs of the North Pacific Indians and the Eskimos.

Almanac

Those *were* the good ol' days and it's always fun to "try to remember the kind of September, when life was slow and oh, so mellow". Those words from the famous song in the musical, "The Fantastiks" really capture the tone of this section, devoted to the past, and a great old mixed bag it is. As the ideas have taken shape we find that whole boutiques can be devoted to this nostalgic theme and many others lend themselves to other promotions within your store. Anniversary sales, Father's Day, Founder's Day and General Store, all are logical possibilities.

Almanac conjures up many colors, smells, textures and memories — all the way from musty leather trunks to fresh crackers and cheese in the old general store. Chicken eggs, candle light, kerosene lamps, tins and gingham are among the images.

The introductory page is a picture of a salesman's sample of the famous Eclipse Iron Stove, loaned by the Niagara Historical Society in Lockport, N.Y. The photos on page 26 are from their collection, as well.

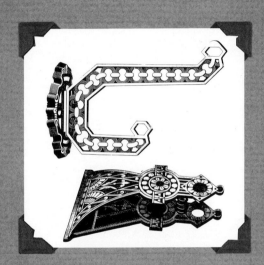

This could be a leaf from an old album. Notice the simple richness of the authentic pieces from door slots to string-holders from the General Store and including a unique apple peeler and a tobacco chopper with a little imp on the handle, thumbing his nose at the world.

This design suggestion offers many possibilities for use as a window display or a central merchandising area for your store in connection with your Almanac or Anniversary promotion. The entire background could be made with pine framing and using 3/16" pebbled Upsonite as surface panels. It can be decorated with many reproductions or painted-on details. The old-fashioned glass front bins could be reproduced using plexi-glass inserts. Authentic looking porcelain and brass pulls are available at hardware stores. Sources for other materials are listed on pages 38-50.

In the Penny Candy Section, starting on page 287, are listed sources for these nice old glass store jars. The old bins and nice country baskets, filled with actual dried corn on the cob are certain to add a country flavor to your promotion. If you are really lucky, you might be able to find one of those beautifully detailed old brass cash registers in the corner of a second hand store.

(If you find two, write and tell us!)

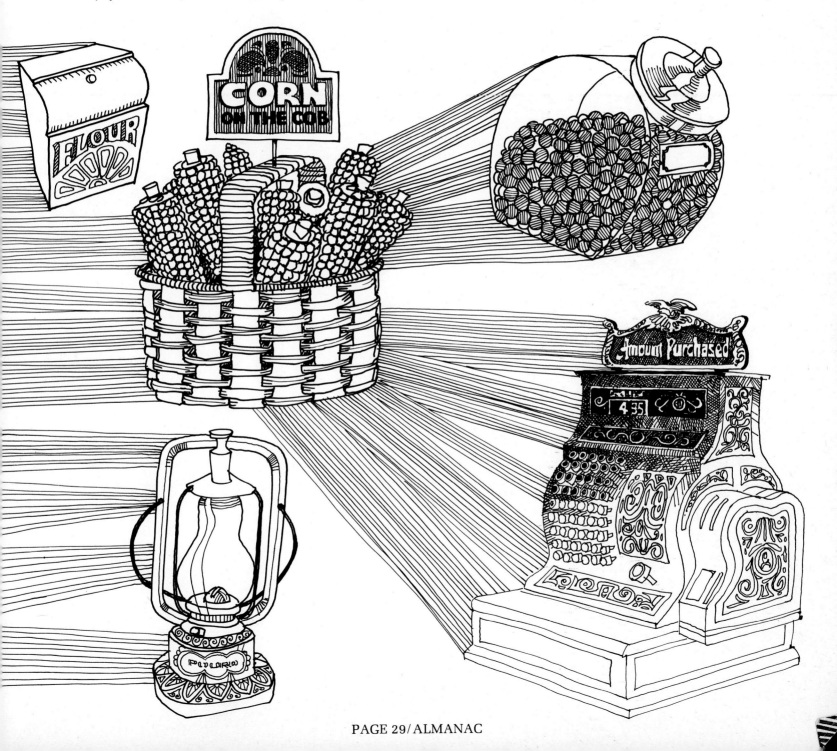

Upson panels can be used in these three display ideas. The Lamp Lighter shop sign could be surface painted. A shelf or bracket could be incorporated into the sign to hold an actual kerosene or reproduction lamp.

FATHER'S DAY RECORD SALE

OLD FASHIONED SEWING MACHINE SALE

LAMPLIGHTER SHOP

EGGS
FARM-FRESH

70th ANNIVERSARY 70th
SALE

WE
GIVE
SATISFACTION

GRANDMA'S
BUTTERMILK

Of all the old-fashioned objects, fireplace bellows seem to provide the greatest potential for a massive central piece for your promotion. They could be built of ⅜″ pebbled Upsonite in two pieces with pine framing added to the edges and imitation leather stretched between the two shapes to form a gigantic six-foot model. These could be hung from the pillars in your store and the shape itself could be used in your newspaper ads and on price tags.

MARTHA'S BATH SHOPPE

The old-fashioned tub with the array of flowers behind it would make a stunning backdrop for your bath shop. For a bath shop wallpiece the print could be enlarged, mounted on Upson Duo-White and the fine detailing around the edges could be accomplished with the Cutawl.

A giant wood-grained washboard would make an eye-catching centerpiece for your January Sale windows. This too, could be made from Upson, which can be wrapped with CONTACT pressure sensitive wallpaper. The ridges are produced with half cut dowels and covered with brass foil contact paper.

The penny farthing Pizza sign has a touch of nostalgia to it and could be used in an antiquated or modern setting. The oversize butcher block proclaiming old-fashioned prices could be used anywhere in your store.

In the Supplier Section, on page 365, are shown additional samples of prints and photos from Culver Pictures Inc. We thought you would enjoy seeing these next four pages to illustrate how fascinating the old stores and shops really were at the end of the last century. These also coincide with our personal fascination with these old stores. They supplement the General Store idea, shown on Page 28.

In the preparation of the Almanac Section we had a great deal of fun finding different supply items that could be used in your display.

On the facing page we have shown four items of interest to you.

Wheaton Products, Millville, New Jersey 08332, has provided two groups of glass items which are ideal for old-fashioned merchandising. In the upper left are shown their LaFayette "Triomphe" storage jars, imported from France. They really have an old-fashioned flavor about them and would make a perfect backdrop effect, filled with coffee beans, cheese, macaroni, etc.

In the lower right hand corner are pictured an assortment of their medicine show bottles. Wheaton resurrected some of the choicest old labels and attached them to clear glass bottles in a variety of shapes and sizes. All come with cork stoppers and vary in size from a three-inch bottle all the way up to 15″ in height.

The used pine nail kegs are from Cordell Enterprises, Inc., 1622 West Morse Ave., Chicago, Illinois 60626. Referring to their correspondence of late 1973, costs of these barrels (12″ diameter by 14″, 17″ and 19″ is approximately $1.25 plus freight). Cordell also carries used oak whiskey barrels, decorator plant tubs, barrel ends, railroad water kegs, etc.

In the lower left hand corner are two of many fascinating items from Phil Papel Imports, Inc., P.O. Box 73718, 8623 S. Mettler St., Los Angeles, Calif. 90003. The larger washboard has two small shelves which can hold merchandise. A complete grouping of these as a background for a January White Sale would be most effective.

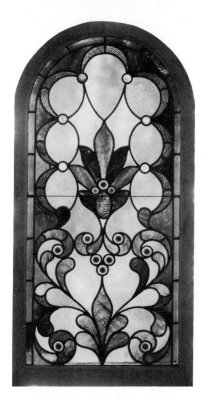

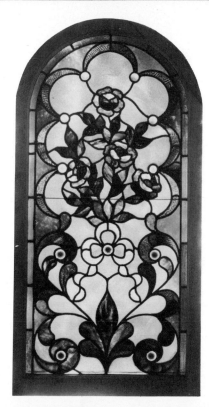

This is just one page of many showing different "one of a kind items" from Gargoyles Limited, 512 S. Third St., Philadelphia 19147. Richard Serbin, who is the Director/Owner of Gargoyles has been most helpful in supplying photographs of many of his interesting items. They have acquired an inventory of good quality stained glass, which in any quantity is difficult to locate. When inquiring about stained glass, please state the following: size required, quantity, predominant colors desired and whether the panel should minimize or maximize transmitted light.

Other items from the Gargoyle collection are shown throughout the book. Their newest catalog is $4.00, available at the address above.

The Cosco collection, Hamilton Cosco Inc., 2225 State Street, Columbus, Indiana 47201, has hundreds of interesting reproductions for all kinds of wall decor. Their African reproductions were described on Page 20 and here are just a few of the dozens available in the American antiques grouping.

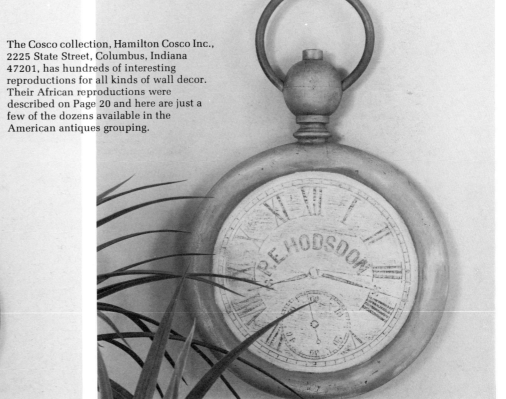

The United House Wrecking Company, 328 Selleck St., Stamford, Conn. 06902, was a joyous discovery. They proudly call their establishment "The Junkyard with a Personality". Here you'll find five acres of relics and nostalgia, more than 30,000 square feet of buildings loaded with furniture, relics from old houses, stained glass, brass and copper, marine salvage, clocks, subway salvage, baker's racks, antiques and just plain junk. 40 minutes from New York City, exit 6 Connecticut Turnpike/right on Harvard Ave.

Write for free literature.

With the energy crisis has come new interest in old stoves and here is a great source for you: Portland Stove Foundry Co., Portland, Maine 04104.

Shown are two models of the classic Franklin Stove and the famous Queen Atlantic. Prices on the Franklins range from $140.00 up and the Queen Atlantic is in the $300.00 range. Write for details.

the yankee heritage collection

In browsing through a shelter magazine we happened upon The Yankee Heritage Collection. It is very unique and the owner, Jerry W. Paner has been most cooperative. The extensive collection covers, not only the kind of merchandise shown here, but also Vermont snow shoe furniture, wooden toys, hand carved signs, doll houses, Maine slate oil paintings, hand crafted weaving looms, carved birds, etc. Their handsome catalog is available by sending 25 cents to P. O. Box 267, Fairfield, Conn. 06430.

The Davos Co., 106 Egel Ave., Middlesex, New Jersey 00846 are designer manufacturers and consultants for Knotwood Advertising display and decorative accessories. They offer a wide range of unusual and interesting blank signs and other fascinating items including the most authentic looking molded split-rail fence that we've seen in a long time.

Here is another firm offering a wide range of molded items for display. The creative boards shown are especially effective and they also offer barn board blanks, bamboo planks and tree trunk planters. Creative Floral Service, 505 W. Monroe St., Chicago, Illinois 60606.

Lucid Lines, 4621 W. Washington Blvd., Los Angeles, 90016, specializes in all kinds of framed glass items and planters. Especially fascinating are authentic pub mirrors reproductions. The Michelob mirror is 16 x 24 and retails for approximately $70. Other trade names are available. Write: Peter Adler, President.

From the famous Jack Daniel Distillery in Tennessee comes a fascinating group of items from the Lynchburg Hardware and General Store, Lynchburg, Tenn. 37352. These items would lend a great deal of authenticity to your Almanac windows and displays. The old time advertising items are of excellent quality and include serving trays, authentic whiskey barrels, tin bottle hanging signs, replicas of old time saloon doors, barnwood frames, walking sticks, ceramic jugs, etc. Direct all inquiries to Mr. Swing.

Concluding the Almanac Section are these clever items from Phil Papel Imports Inc., P.O. Box 73718, 8623 S. Mettler St., Los Angeles, California 90003. The full line runs from burnt wood mirrors and plaques to chamber pots, mugs and the assorted wash boards also shown on page 38. Write for current items and prices.

AMERICAN

Some of the most unique and original designs produced in the United States were developed by the American Indian. Our design group has been especially fascinated with the architecture and designs of the Indians of the Mountains and Mesas of the far West.

The cliff-dwelling Pueblos in New Mexico were visited in 1540 by the Spanish Explorer, Coronado, and soon Spanish settlers began arriving in New Mexico. After the Pueblos came the Nomads of Mesas, the Apaches, the Navajos, Commanches and others. From these great tribes come ancient symbolic designs, which were used on trays, masks, pewter, Kachina dolls, shawls, blankets, etc.

The beauty of this design heritage has been combined with the architectural style taken from the Taos Adobes. Adobe has an Arabic origin meaning, "Earth from which unburnt bricks are made." The bricks were a balanced mixture of clay and sand; not enough sand to keep the dry clay from cracking, but enough clay to give the dried mixture strength.

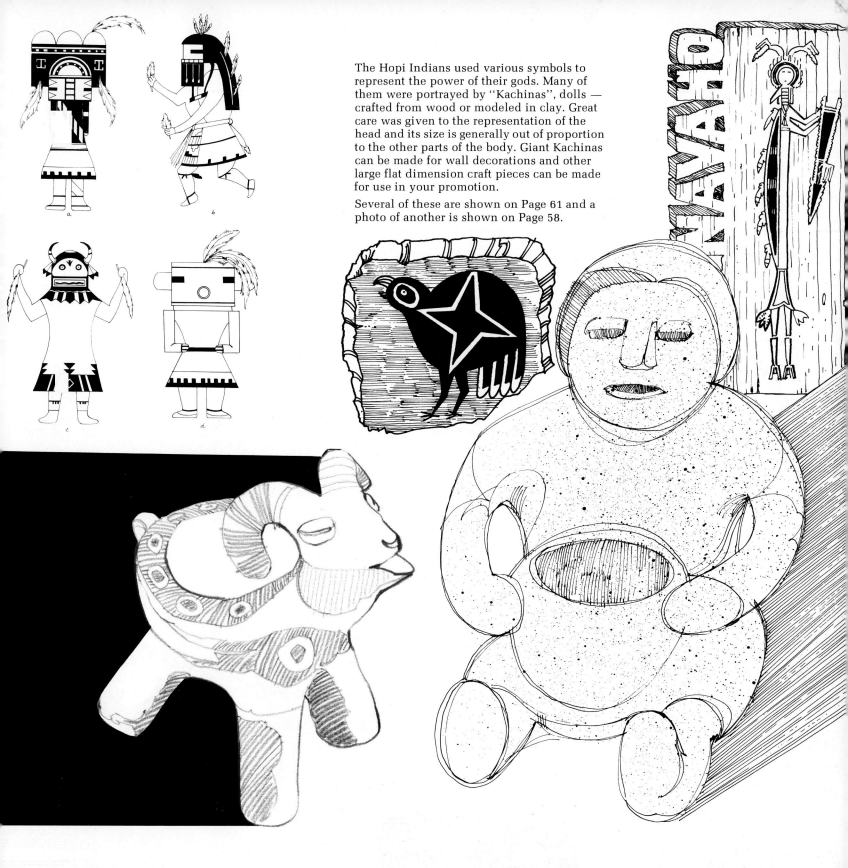

The Hopi Indians used various symbols to represent the power of their gods. Many of them were portrayed by "Kachinas", dolls — crafted from wood or modeled in clay. Great care was given to the representation of the head and its size is generally out of proportion to the other parts of the body. Giant Kachinas can be made for wall decorations and other large flat dimension craft pieces can be made for use in your promotion.

Several of these are shown on Page 61 and a photo of another is shown on Page 58.

NAVAHO

Realizing that the Adobe structures are basically simple in construction, we feel the use of Upson ⅜″ All Weather Panels with thick texture paint covering will make an authentic looking facade or individual Adobe arts and crafts section in your store. The architectural detail can be produced with different thicknesses of Upson.

The rough hewn timbers can be produced by staining the Upson in dark brown, highlights can be achieved by an even darker brown, using a natural sponge. Elaborate filigree for use over portals can be produced with ¼″ Upson, using a Stanley knife or a Cutawl.

CONSTRUCTION DETAILS

A. Doorway — A simple classic door with rough-hewn woodwork.

B. A west elevation of the Jose Maria Martinez House in Taos, New Mexico.

C. The Spanish constructed roofs in much the same fashion as the Indians, by spanning the interior space with Vigas (horizontal beams) and allowing the ends of the Vigas to protrude through the exterior walls.

D. Spanish-built walls are characteristically thick, about eighteen inches to two feet, producing the distinct "thick look".

E. This profile of a pediment on the door to the Salita Oscura Adobe, reflects the distinctive Spanish influence.

F. In pre-Spanish times, the Indians laid small saplings across the Vigas. These were called, "Latias" by the Spanish, when they used this technique. Sometimes they were arranged in a herring-bone pattern and often were painted different colors.

G. The Valdez House in Taos is an excellent example of Spanish colonial architecture and this detail of the portal lintel shows this influence.

H. The scroll work in the trim on the portal of the Martinez house is an excellent example of ingenious jig-saw work of the facia at the eave line.

I. Following the Spanish influence many of the walls contained niches to hold pottery.

Countless authentic Navajo crafts are available from the Navajo Nation and Martin Link, Department Head, Museum and Research of the Navajo Nation, Window Rock, Ariz. 86515, is a helpful and enthusiastic source. Mr. Link described the kind of authentic Navajo rug and jewelry, Pueblo pottery, baskets and Kachinas offered in their museum shop. The photos on page 58 illustrate the beautiful quality and craftsmanship of these items and we suggest that you stop when you are in the area, to see this most interesting museum and shop.

As we mentioned earlier, Dover Publications, 180 Varick St., New York 10014, has been most helpful in allowing reproduction of the pages from a wide assortment of their excellent reference books. On the next three pages are shown dozens of line drawings from their book, "American Indian Design and Decoration" by Leroy H. Appleton and we highly recommend it. The entire book provides hundreds of authentic decorative designs, which in turn, can be converted into giant decor pieces, border treatments and general reference for your American Adobe promotion.

AMERICAN
INDIAN
DESIGN &
DECORATION
LE ROY H. APPLETON
WITH OVER 700 ILLUSTRATIONS
FROM THE ENTIRE WESTERN HEMISPHERE

HOPI CEREMONIAL BLANKET

WOMAN'S DRESS, ACOMA

HOPI WEDDING SHAWL

WOMAN'S DRESS, ACOMA

NAVAHO BLANKET

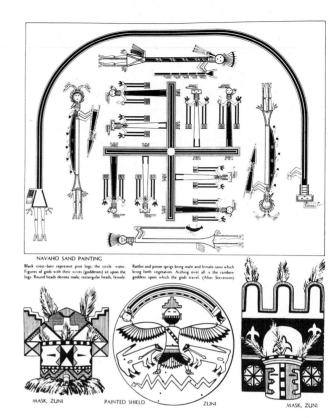

NAVAHO SAND PAINTING

Black cross-bars represent pine logs; the circle water. Figures of gods with their wives (goddesses) sit upon the logs. Round heads denote male; rectangular heads, female. Rattles and pinon sprigs bring male and female rains which bring forth vegetation. Arching over all is the rainbow goddess upon which the gods travel. (After Stevenson)

MASK, ZUNI   PAINTED SHIELD   ZUNI   MASK, ZUNI

REPRESENTATIVE UNITS AND SYMBOLS

LIGHTNING

CLOUDS AND RAIN

CLOUD

RAINBOW

CLOUDS

SUN

ALTAR WITH FEATHERS

SUN   FLOWER

EXIT TRAIL OF LIFE

COUGAR AND CARDINAL POINTS

BIRDS

BIRD HANGING FROM SKY BAND

THUNDER-BIRD

BIRDS

BIRDS

BUTTERFLY

CLOUD SERPENTS

PLUMED SERPENT

RAIN SERPENT

DEER

WORM (ON BASKET)

TURTLE   LION

CORN

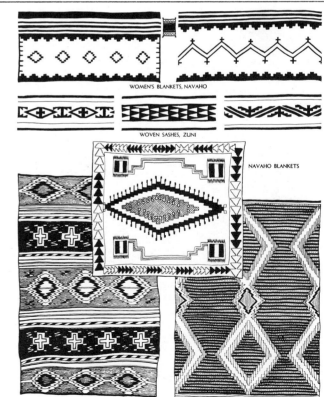

WOMEN'S BLANKETS, NAVAHO

WOVEN SASHES, ZUNI

NAVAHO BLANKETS

SILVER AND TURQUOISE ZUNI

HOPI KACHINA
(AFTER WATERCOLOR
PAINTING BY FRED KABOTI)

HOPI KACHINA

NAVAHO

TRAY, HOPI

BEADWORK
MESCALERO
APACHE

KACHINA TRAY
HOPI

TURQUOISE AND
SHELL MOSAIC
ARIZONA

HIDE MASK, ZUNI

HIDE MASK, ZUNI

COCHITI

PUEBLO   POTTERY

SAN JUAN

CASAS GRANDES

HAWIKUH

CASAS GRANDES

HAWIKUH

SANTA ANA

CASAS GRANDES

SAN ILDEFONSO

SIA

ACOMA

ZUNI

MIMBRES   POTTERY

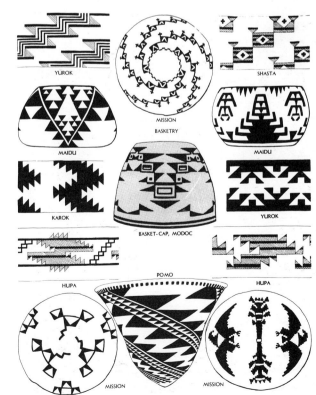

YUROK

MISSION
BASKETRY

SHASTA

MAIDU

MAIDU

KAROK

YUROK

BASKET-CAP, MODOC

HUPA

POMO

HUPA

MISSION

MISSION

CLIFF-DWELLINGS AND PUEBLO POTTERY

MOTIVE FROM LAGUNA JAR

ACOMA

MOTIVE FROM LAGUNA JAR

SAN ILDEFONSO

ZUNI

PUEBLO   ZUNI   POTTERY

ZUNI   ZUNI

MOTIVE FROM ZUNI JAR   ZUNI   MOTIVE FROM ZUNI JAR

BASKETS   AND TRAYS

WHITE MOUNTAIN APACHE   WHITE MOUNTAIN APACHE

HOPI POTTERY

PIMA   PIMA

JICARILLA APACHE   HOPI   MESCALERO APACHE

HAVASUPAI   PIMA

PUEBLO POTTERY

ACOMA

SANTO DOMINGO   SAN ILDEFONSO

ACOMA

SANTO DOMINGO   LAGUNA

ZUNI

SIA   SIA   ACOMA

PAGE 62/AMERICAN ADOBE

Art Deco is the name generally applied to the typical art production of the 1920's and 30's. The name is derived from the Exposition Internationale des Arts Decoratifs et Industriels Modernes. The art of that period was extremely varied and its sources included turn-of-the-century Art Nouveau.

Most of the important artistic movements followed: Cubism, Futurism and Expressionism, it was also influenced by Ancient Egyptian and Mayan Art. Art Deco has been rediscovered with tremendous impact. Authorities agree that Art Deco is more symmetrical than asymmetrical and more gracefully geometric than its undulating, voluptuously rendered predecessor, Art Nouveau.

With this new interest our Section offers a few display and promotional ideas. On page 65, we have designed a simple boutique floor plan, using Art Deco motifs, dividers and merchandise racks.

BOUTIQUE

Antoni Gaudi (1852-1926) was Barcelona's greatest master of Art Nouveau. The son of an iron worker, Gaudi was born in Reus. As a boy, he practiced his father's craft and this early training is evident in many of Gaudi's later works. He produced scores of unusual buildings and churches, the most famous of which was the church of Sagrada Familia.

The form shown on this page is derived from his stained glass windows in the chapel of the Colonia Güell and it would make a beautiful central piece for your constructions. From the standpoint of design and construction, you will be fascinated by studying the designs of his structures, furniture, railings and decor. Among the most curious and yet charming ideas were the serpentine benches, decorated with bits of tiles, pottery, shards and pieces of marble, done in mosaic style that resembled the scaly body of a great snake or lizard.

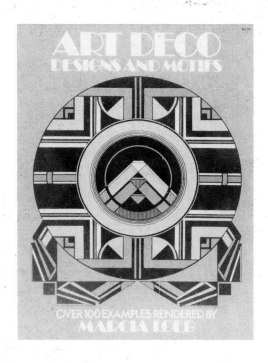

Again, we have reproduced some pages from another Dover Publication on Art Deco and design motifs rendered by Marcia Loeb. This book is a collection of 75 plates offering over 100 Art Deco designs, based on samples from many branches of the arts including, fabrics, stained glass, furniture, metal work and architecture. You will find it a helpful reference guide when planning your Art Deco display.

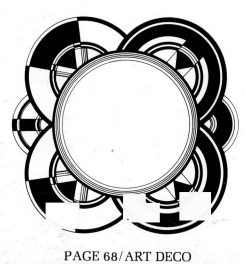

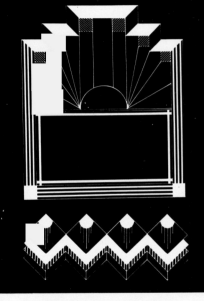

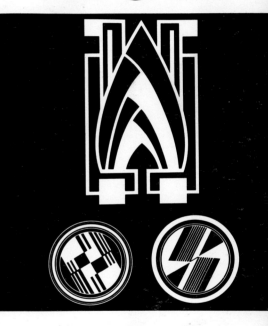
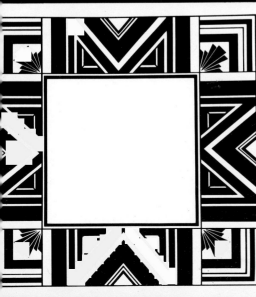
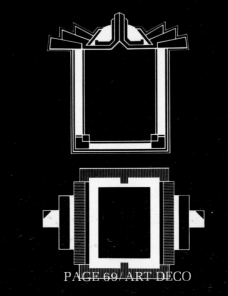

In our Almanac Section on Page 47, we featured three framed Pub Mirrors from Lucid Lines of Los Angeles. The two that are illustrated here are from their French Art Nouveau grouping. These bronze framed pictures are screened on glass in multi-colors and mounted away from the background to produce a three dimensional effect. Lucid Lines offers a wide variety of objects, not only in regular framed prints, but in hanging planters, as well.

Lucid Lines, 4621 W. Washington Blvd., Los Angeles, Calif. 90016

Skiing has become a popular sport throughout many parts of the country. On the next three pages are some display ideas for whole departments and for individual signs and displays.

ASPEN

SKI PLAYGROUND

SPORTSWEAR

ACTUAL OR DUMMY BOOT PLACED ON PLATFORM IN CUT-OUT SHAPE.

SKI SHOP

SKI FEVER

Using ³/₁₆ Pebbled Upson board, this ski-wear merchandiser was designed using the shape of the ski as our design form. Simple sliding door cabinets can be constructed below, or just the ski shape motif could be used for a window display. The snowflake sign can be handled in many different ways. It could be constructed of different thicknesses of Upson, painted with Illinois Bronze's wet-look paints and used above a shop doorway, or the outside form can be made from pine framing and Upson "skins". It could be lighted from the inside and a stained glass effect achieved by using colored cellophane on plexiglass with artificial leading.

Webster described the Atrium as the center of a Roman House and we have adapted this concept to form a shop with beautiful Roman atmosphere. The merchandising possibilities are unlimited. It could be a combination of small shops or the entire structure could be devoted to a clothes boutique or gift shop.

ATRIUM

ATRIUM

Many forms come to mind in designing for this period. Deep dimensional Warriors, Roman helmets and columns can all be formed in flat or two dimensional forms.

Many supplier items are available for use in producing your Roman Shop. Although they are sometimes difficult to find, large lumber stores carry pressed wooden moldings with egg and dart and scroll patterns. The bracket in the lower right hand corner is available from Jo Mead Designs, 17 N. Elizabeth St., Chicago, Ill. 60607.

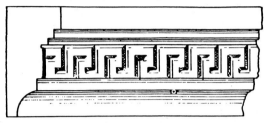

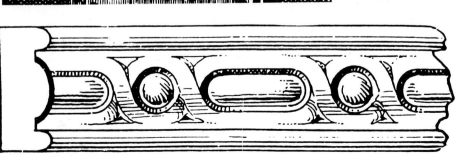

The Silvestri Studio, 1733 Cordova St., Los Angeles, 90007, produces a beautiful line of Vitriglas objects, featuring a fascinating pitted or "Travertine" finish that makes these productions look richly authentic. Silvestri offers hundreds of different items. We have shown just a few selections in the Roman style, which might be used in connection with your Atrium promotion. To give you an idea of cost, the wholesale price for the Lyceum horses plaque (24″ h. x 30″ w.) is approximately $35.

Write to Silvestri for current prices and selections.

We discovered a little ad for Focal Point Inc., 1760 S. Roswell Rd., Rte. 3, Marietta, Ga. 30060, in House & Garden magazine. Focal Point is engaged in reproducing well-designed, hand-crafted architectural work, both period and modern.

The original is re-engineered by model and mold-makers and then the production mold is made, making possible the reproducing in modern polymers of every crisp detail. On the opposite page we have shown four of their beautiful ceiling medallions. No. 801 in the upper left hand corner is 8½″ in diameter and No. 802 in the lower right hand corner is 30″ in diameter. On this page we have shown several cornice moldings and the beautifully designed Niche cap and casings. All items can be stained and are extremely lightweight for shipping.

Write Focal Point for additional details.

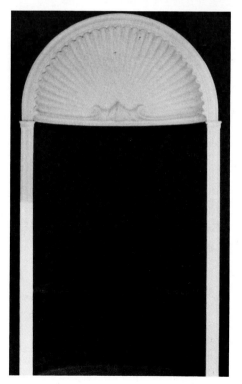

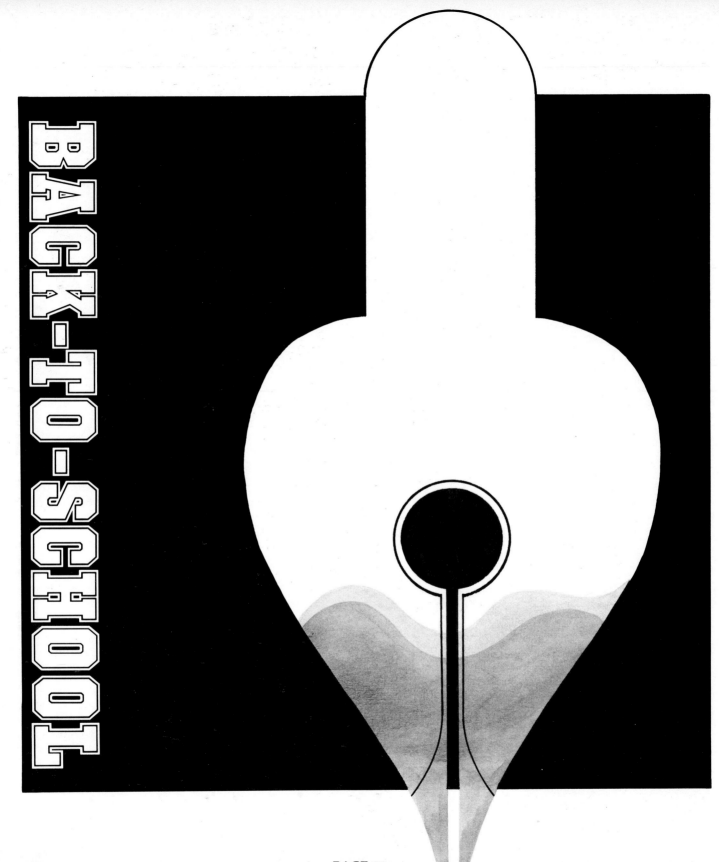

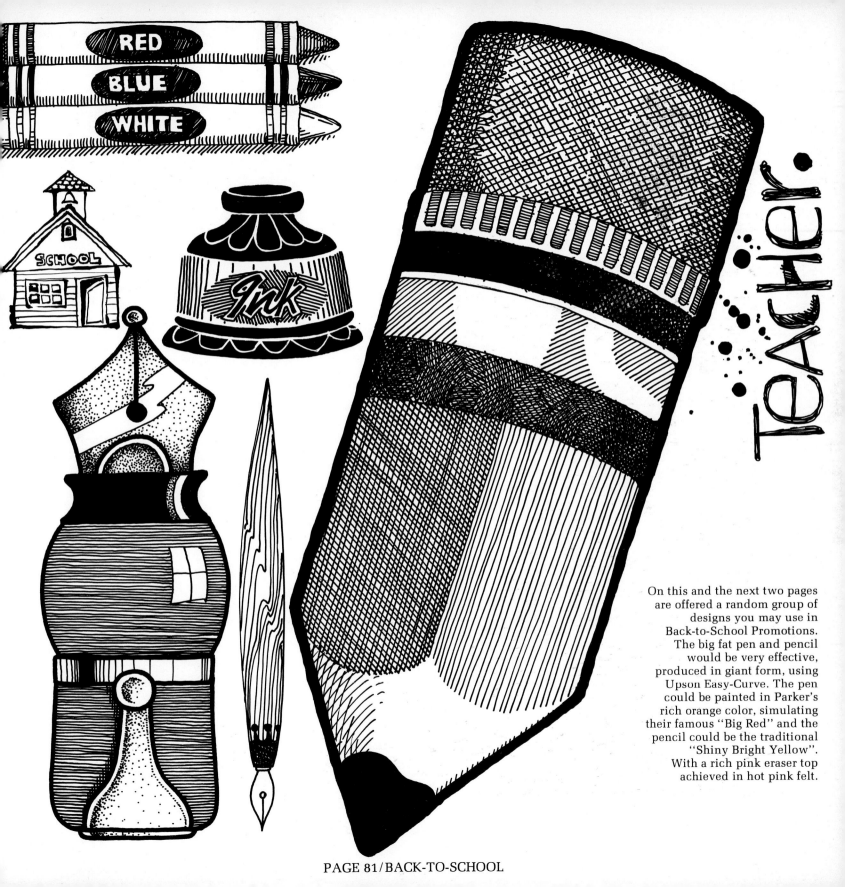

RED
BLUE
WHITE

SCHOOL

Ink

TeAcHeR

On this and the next two pages are offered a random group of designs you may use in Back-to-School Promotions. The big fat pen and pencil would be very effective, produced in giant form, using Upson Easy-Curve. The pen could be painted in Parker's rich orange color, simulating their famous "Big Red" and the pencil could be the traditional "Shiny Bright Yellow". With a rich pink eraser top achieved in hot pink felt.

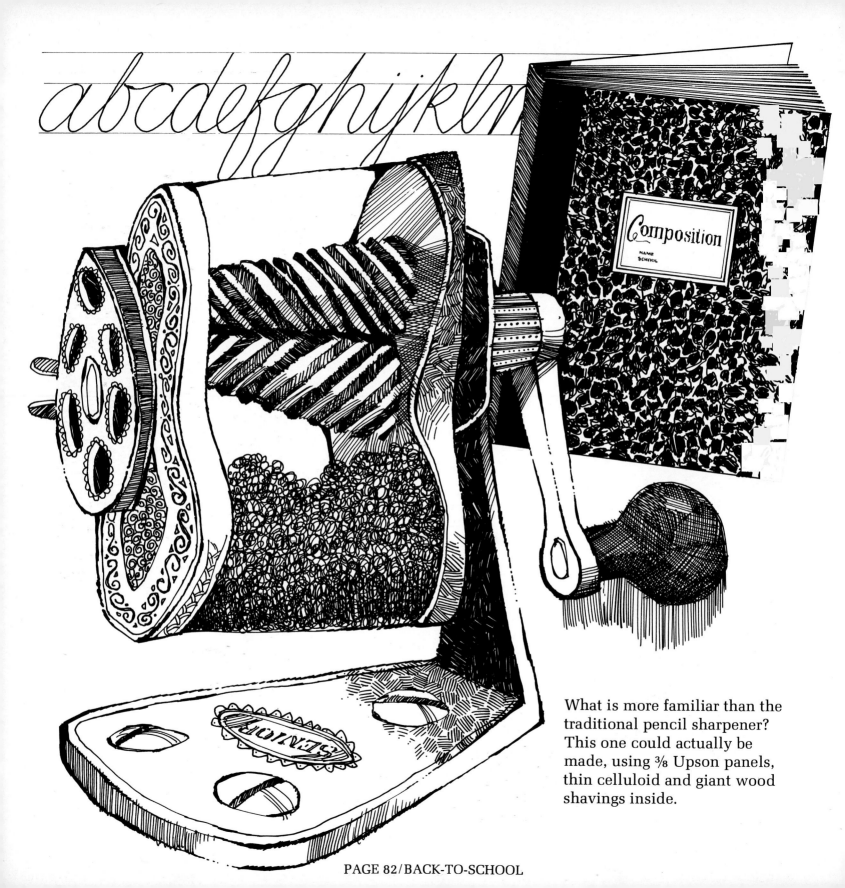

What is more familiar than the traditional pencil sharpener? This one could actually be made, using ⅜ Upson panels, thin celluloid and giant wood shavings inside.

BANNERS

and other neat hanging things.

Banners

Quoting from Norman La Liberte's book "Banners and Hangings" we find that in 1555 a famous procession was held in Florence. In that procession Sienese military companies each carried their own banner. Banners and hangings as we know them today originated there and then moved to Rome, where they became battle insignia.

During the Crusades, banners and flags came into widespread use and heraldic flags developed their great variety during the Middle Ages. During that time merchants and craft guilds each developed an identifying banner and from this have developed all kinds of designs, announcing international functions and pageants. The design and material possibilities are unlimited. On the following pages we offer some ideas and as one design indicates on page 88, banners are a great way to fill large open areas.

BOOTIQUE

AUTUMN

SALE

A great way to fill large open areas and cover ugly ceiling voids

KITCHEN KRAFT

ANTIQUE AUCTION

SWAP SHOP

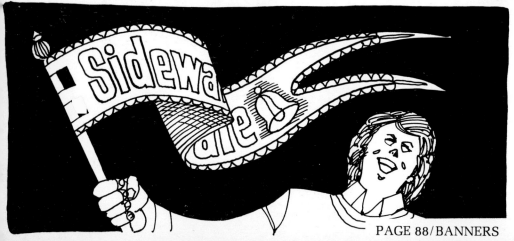

Sidewalk Sale

PEACE

Culver Prints in New York has supplied these beautiful line drawings to show how banners have played an important part in history. Please remember these Culver prints were loaned to us and should not be reproduced without consulting Culver Prints for reproduction fees.

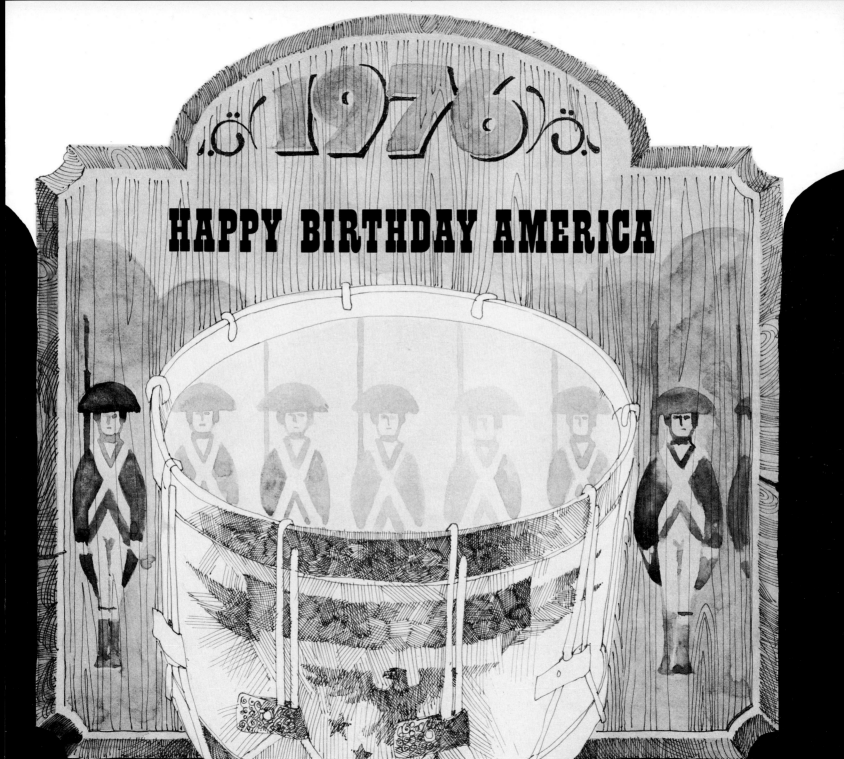

On March 1, 1975, the United States of America officially begins the celebration of its 200th Anniversary. From a display and promotional standpoint it's the perfect promotion that can involve all areas within your store. On the next few pages we are pleased to present a few display and promotional ideas. Following them are a collection of sign ideas and supplier information.

Needless to say, many manufacturers will be producing Bi-Centennial merchandise for this important national observance.

In collecting the material for these pages we became intrigued with the promotional possibilities. We are convinced the real key to your promotion will be local "tie-ins". Your own Museum and Historical Society have a great deal to offer, loaning actual local treasures, and providing research and inspiration to your designers.

ALL IS WELL

1776-1976

USE COLONIAL-TYPE STRUCTURE FOR MERCHANDISE ISLAND DISPLAY.

Our central unit takes it's influence from Independence Hall. Your Bi-Centennial Promotion will carry more impact if you use the designs of local structures and regional historical figures. This structure can be constructed of pine framing with 3/16 pebbled Upson covered with printed or plastic embossed brick panels. The detail and filigree can be achieved with the Cutawl.

In developing plans for your celebration, it might be very effective to construct, both inside and outside of your store, a street of shops made to resemble a street in your city or town as it was in the 18th Century. Certainly this will be easier for those of you whose cities were in the Original 13 Colonies. Research collected from your local historical societies will help, aided by any prints, city plans and pages from archives, showing how buildings looked at that time in your community.

B.F. ANDERSON, TOBACCONIST

Colonial-type buildings

The street of shops concept is not a new idea, but it is effective. For your Bi-Centennial structures the ideal panel to use for exterior facing would be ⅜″ Upson All Weather. This panel is versatile for the following reasons: It's strong (⅜″ laminated construction), water-proof and best of all it will take many different mediums. It can be painted to simulate a brick facade or All Weather can be lightly textured to resemble the stucco houses of the period. It may also be applied to resemble colonial lap-sided fronts. The weather beaten, sun-silvered look will give your structures real authenticity.

Christmas at
Mount Vernon could be
the basis of a full promotion at
Christmas time and the six paneled
display below could be
educational as well as a
stunning divider in
your store.

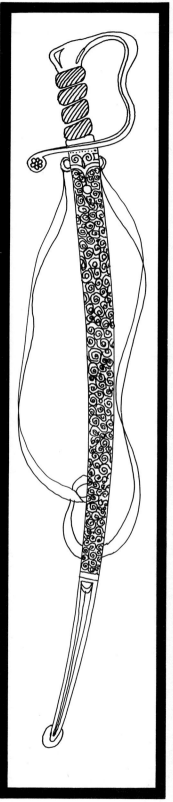

Eagles of all styles and constructions will certainly be one of the dominant design elements in the Bi-Centennial promotions and the powdered wigs of colonial times could also be made in giant form. We suggest a huge 8 foot wig of manila rope, glued and wired to the Upson background to form a smart backdrop for your display windows.

Mitten's Design Letters, 85 Fifth Avenue, New York 10003, was one of the first firms to present Bi-Centennial ideas to the National Association of Display Industries. We present for your pleasure the following 30 sign and display ideas, based on the colonial theme and incorporating their deep dimension letters of all styles and sizes. For information on the complete line write to Mitten's in New York.

The Tinsmith sign combines an old hame, walnut wood plaque and small tin cookie cutters. The Bi-Centennial U.S.A. sign incorporates a prepainted plaque with Mitten's Letters. An antique brass key adds dimension to the Christmas in Williamsburg plaque.

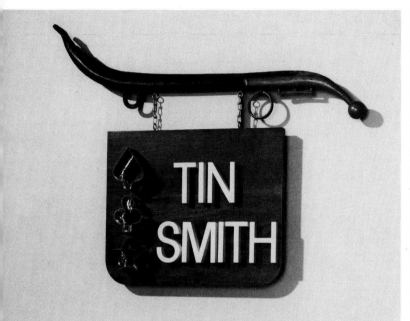

The Washington Shop has been formed with felt covered Upson shapes and uses as a final touch colonial style brass buttons. The Mug and Musket is made of stained basswood. Mitten's Showboat letters and a dimensional pistol lend a rich feeling of history to this pedestal sign.

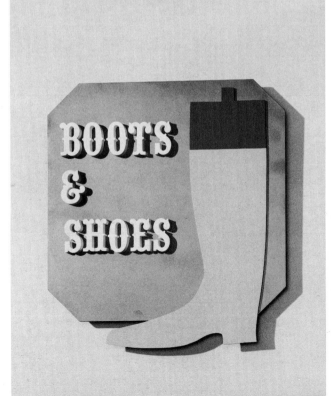

The Brass Buckle sign is actually a big buckle cut from polished sheet brass with Mitten's Vista letters in the center. To the right of this we show how effectively 2″ Montclair Standee letters can be used to form a Sale sign. The wig was made with white yarn.

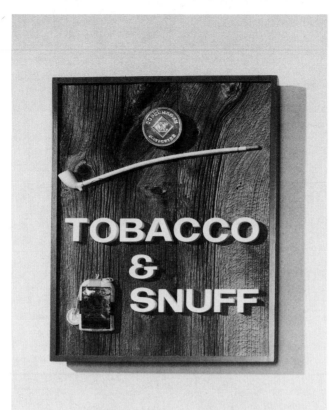

The richly embossed piece of actual barn board, an old fashioned clay churchwarden pipe and two packages of tobacco complete this colonial montage. The shadow box with shelves was made from the casing of a pine clock box. A giant "T" in Mitten's Montclair series forms the base for this "play-on-words".

Many stores carry beautiful models of colonial soldiers, which are ideal for small window displays. The Colonial Originals; uses as its central piece a pre-painted pine sign with the names of the 13 original states; formed in waves below it.

Montclair Standee numerals rest on the shelves formed by this deep dimensional star and The Quill is an appropriate name for your Christmas Stationery Shop.

The sign of the Holly was made from Upson All Weather fibreboard with a sand textured paint applied to simulate the old tudor walls of English Inns. It could be the name of a colonial shop selling trims and ornaments. Regular manila rope with its natural hemp color forms this stunning seacoast sign idea.

The Hearthside is a combination of Mitten's Letters, plastic fake bricks and one of Yorkraft's standard colonial sign boards (33½" x 22") painted in a rich cocoa brown. The Colonial Christmas Belles and The Brass Button are both formed of felt covered Upson panels.

Yorkraft, Inc., 550 S. Pine St., York, Penna. 17405, has produced a catalog illustrating the wall decorations and accessories inspired by America's past. The items are especially interesting at this time, with the Bi-Centennial promotions underway. We have shown only seven of approximately 200 ideas.

Just before we went to press we made a happy discovery. We found that the Newspaper Advertising Bureau Inc., 485 Lexington Avenue, N.Y., N.Y. 10017 has produced an amazing handbook, designed to help retailers build promotions and newspaper campaigns around the Bi-Centennial celebration. The book's title is "The Spirit of '76" in 4 color format, 12" x 16" — 64 pages. Five full pages are the work of Fred Otnus, highlighting sections of the book. The first part is a historical background of the Revolutionary period, covering the people, how they lived, the War, the Press, Trivia and quotes from the lighter side of our early days. Pages 42 thru 55 are a work book section, featuring black and white advertising borders and clip art (some examples are shown below) and we feel it's one of the best selections of reproduction art, produced for the Bi-Centennial.

The final section of the book includes promotional ideas for retailers, information on the government's Bi-Centennial network.

E. Lawrence Goodman, Vice President, informs us that the book is available for $7.50 per copy to anyone except retailers. Qualified retailers can obtain their own copy from local newspapers.

Noble and Cooley Co. specializes in reproductions of colonial drums in the form of waste baskets, small tables, hassocks, etc. Illustrated are just two of their very complete line. The display possibilities are unlimited. Groups of these could be used in window displays, the hassocks could be used for actual seating in one of your Bi-Centennial boutiques and used singly, that could hold other colonial merchandise.

Contact Robert A. Hill Inc., 225 Fifth Ave., New York 10010

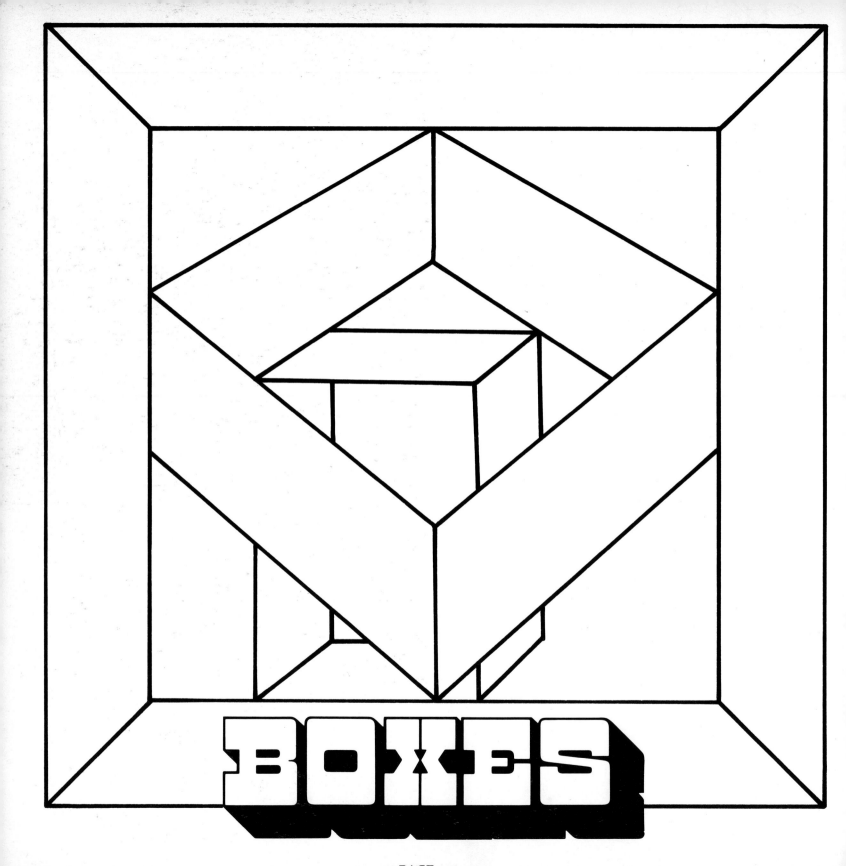

From this classic form all kinds of great possibilities for structural and decorative treatments can be developed. The basic structure can be created in many ways and the box need not be completely square. It can be elongated or stacked; made big or small and fitted into different and sometimes difficult spaces. Stack them, use them as a base for shelves, let them be open on two ends, even light them from inside. Try them with clear plastic sheets as a surface with detail line work, including plastic cut-out letters, actual dimensional objects, etc.

Wouldn't a giant box, open on one end and completely lined with tiny mirrors be a spectacular way to show a new line of fashions? Upson-covered frames can form all kinds of animals, clowns, and just plain display cubes.

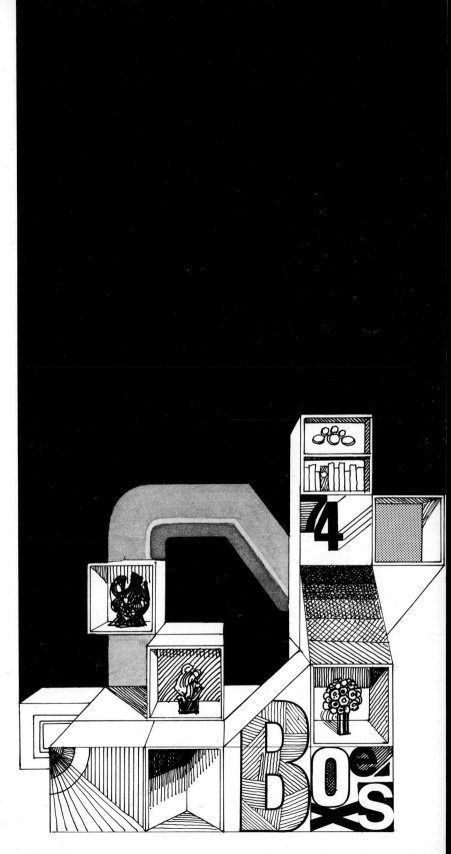

Why not form a square apple, using Upson panels decorated in shiny bright red paint with a snappy leaf and stem coming from the middle?

And a form in the shape of a folding box with your retail message?

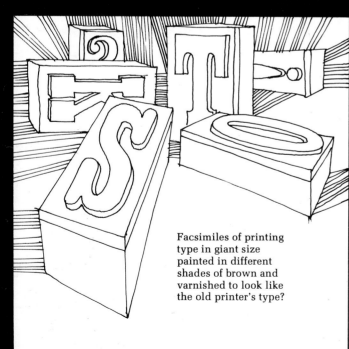

Facsimiles of printing type in giant size painted in different shades of brown and varnished to look like the old printer's type?

And a simple cubed display.

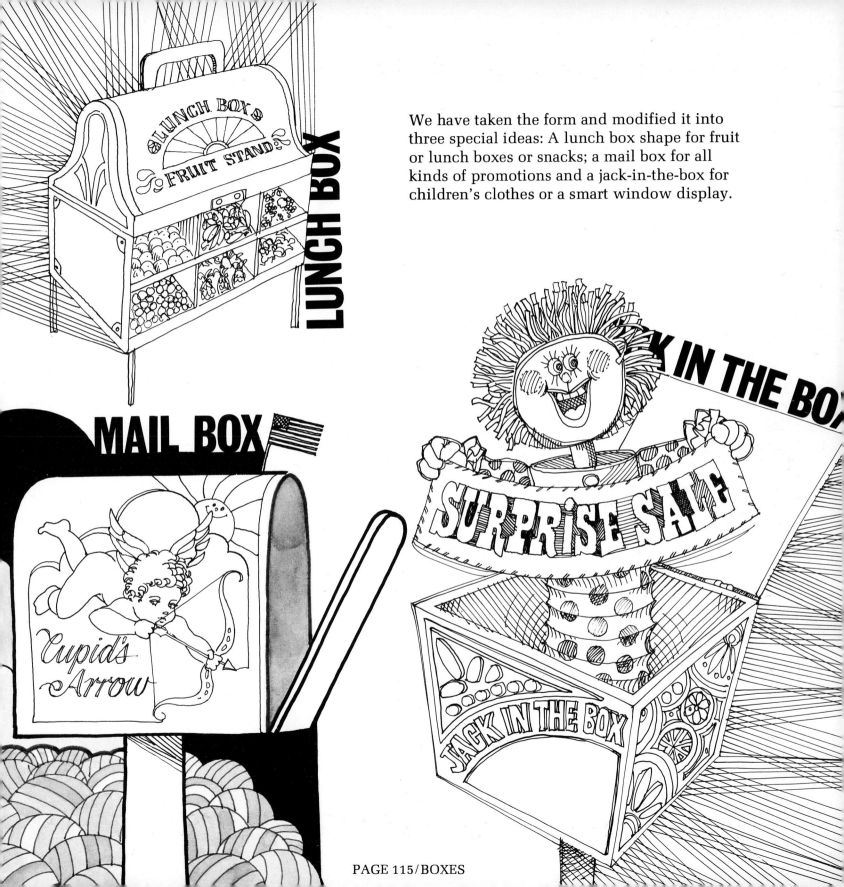

LUNCH BOX

We have taken the form and modified it into three special ideas: A lunch box shape for fruit or lunch boxes or snacks; a mail box for all kinds of promotions and a jack-in-the-box for children's clothes or a smart window display.

MAIL BOX

JACK IN THE BOX

Originally, this design
was part of our
Kidsworld Section,
starting on page 241.
In essence it is a box
idea for a children's
department, for toys or
a "look-in" attention
getter.

TOY WONDERLAND

TAKE A PEEK INTO A MAGICAL LAND

The basic box shape has been transformed into a display for farm produce, a beautiful trolley car done in 3/16 pebbled Upsonite and a series of hanging boxes for all kinds of promotions.

FARM PRODUCE

I'M A LiTTLE FiSH AND I'M MADE FROM A BOX. I CAN BE A BIRD, OR AN ELEPHANT, OR ANYTHING. IT'S FUN JUST HANGING AROUND

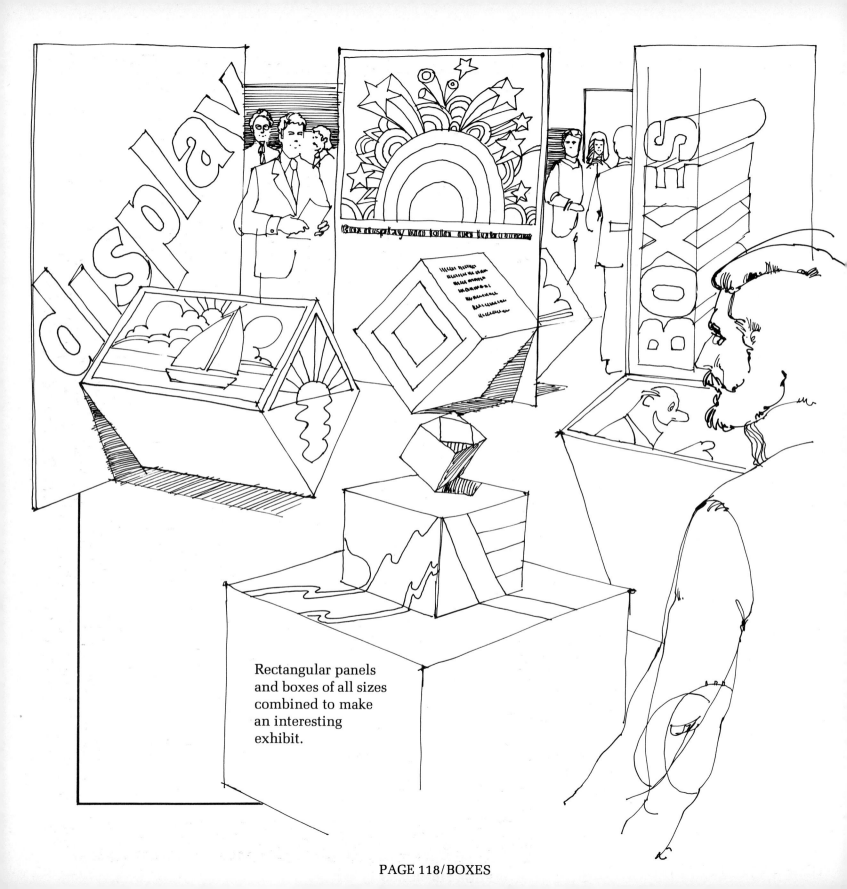

Rectangular panels
and boxes of all sizes
combined to make
an interesting
exhibit.

These beautiful designs
are from a great series of
small window displays
for Tiffany's in New York
City, using wooden
shapes, antique doll parts,
spindles and balls.

Four beautiful examples of decorative items from Ye Unicorne represented by Faroy Sales, 1133 Dallas Trade Mart, Dallas, 75207. (They also have a show room in New York at 225 Fifth Avenue, Room 731). The kitchen decor boxes are very smart and were produced in Baker's dough with gingham backgrounds. The Turn of the Century Pasta box retails for around $20.

The printer's type drawer in the lower right hand corner is filled with memorabilia. These are available at local flea markets and "The Junk Yard with a Personality" mentioned in the Almanac Section on page 42.

The two other illustrations were furnished by Illinois Bronze and illustrate how beautifully decoupage and Vue d'optique, (the French method of producing optical illusions with the use of three identical prints) can work in displays.

WHITE
ON
WHITE

CHRISTMAS
IN ALL DIRECTIONS

This group of Christmas ideas have tremendous possibilities. The joy structure on the left hand corner of Page 122 could be a big panel of Upson with the letters cut out to form a divider for a department within your store.

Christmas in All Directions is self-explanatory. Two ideas that might be used for an unusual approach to your Christmas promotions are the giant bubble ice cream cone produced with Upson panels and foil. They could be a central design theme for your promotion and the Christmas formed of stacked heart shapes could also be used to great advantage. This too, could be produced in bright pink foil or mylar or the hearts could be covered in one of our favorite display materials, shocking or hot pink felt from Allied Felt, 24 W. 25th Street, New York 10010.

A gigantic glove shape in felt on 3/8 Upson in bright colors, with a period motif.

A rocking horse Santa in giant form for a window, in light-weight form for hanging or on top of island counters.

A beautiful shiny harmonica to hang over a counter, featuring musical Christmas gifts.

A traditional puppet Santa in natural wood with dowel pegs.

A Caroler in dimensional form.

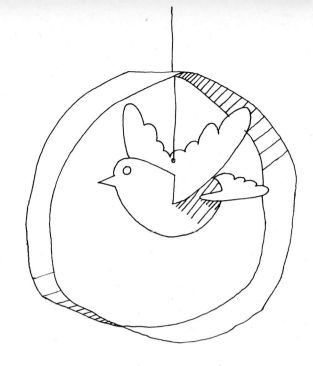

Huge bird mobile in foil and
Upson Easy-Curve.

Christmas Mailbox.

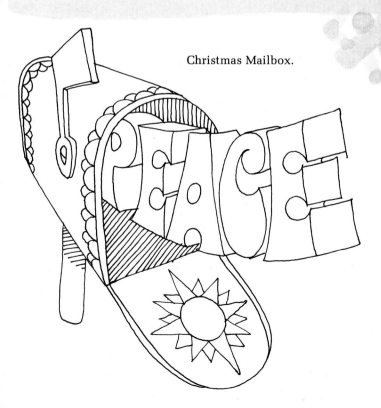

And the first-cousin of our
circus character on Page
115, a Christmas
Jack-in-the-box.

WRAPPING PAPER

The inter-lock idea can be used very effectively with this simple treeshape decorated in any number of ways — bright Mexican colors, lacquered to a shiny finish or produced in dimensional form with various thicknesses of Upson.

The western Santa is a favorite and could be used as a massive piece, towering 12′ or 15′ in the air as a dramatic focal point for Christmas in the West.

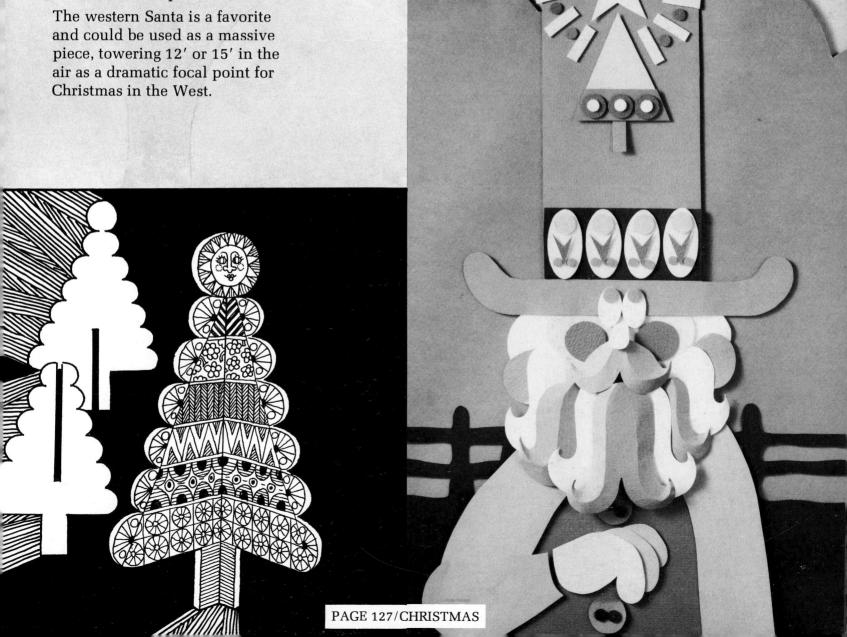

Dimensional shapes to form shelves have always been used at Christmas and we present for your consideration three different ideas.

The circular shapes can be made from Upson Easy-Curve cylinders or sections of fibreboard tubing. The shelves on the triangular shaped tree can hold beautiful ornaments under each leading edge. We especially like the partridge in a pear tree form that could be reproduced in different sizes throughout the store; in small scale, for small windows, in large size for housewares and gifts departments.

Six creative designs for the holidays. The most original, a partridge in a pear tree form for use throughout the store.

PEACE ON EARTH

DECEMBER

25

Deep dimensional forms can be used throughout the store and two on the left can be used effectively as large window pieces or in smaller scale. The tower design could be converted in a "Visit with Santa" platform with bright felt cones, banners and large gold Christmas trim.

The fish has long been a religious symbol connected with Christmas and this one can be made from a large panel of Upson board with some forms cut all the way through and lighted from behind. The ribbon candy form is produced from a slice of a paper tube and large ribbon or colored paper.

There is something fascinating about the classic form of an orange crate. This shape has been combined with a dimensional sun and Mitten's Letters on an orange disc.

In the tradition of peasant folk art, we have designed some simple wooden base figures for use throughout the store. Beautifully detailed cake forms can be made from Upson Easy Curve and sprayed with silver paint or covered with household foil or Mylar sheets, available from local display houses.

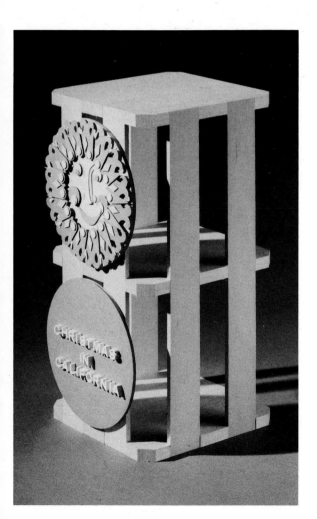

Take a giant ball, slice it in half, add some shelves and some crisp bright details on the outside and you have a spectacular Christmas Corner in the form of a huge ornament. The basic form can be made of pine framing, with chicken wire holding the papier-maché outer covering.

This beautifully ornamented Santa could serve as the main theme for your entire Christmas promotion. Imagine him in huge form decorated in all kinds of trim, felt, bells, bangles and beads. Four panels of Upson in 4 x 8 size will produce the giant.

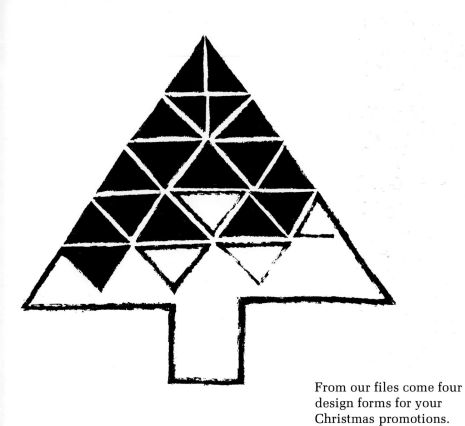

From our files come four
design forms for your
Christmas promotions.
The elaborate tree print is
from the Bettman
Archive, 136 East 57th
St., New York 10022.

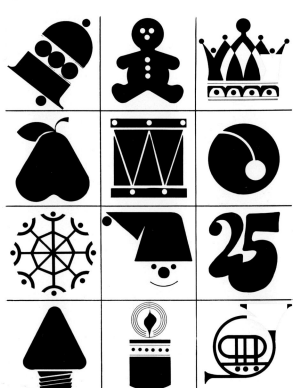

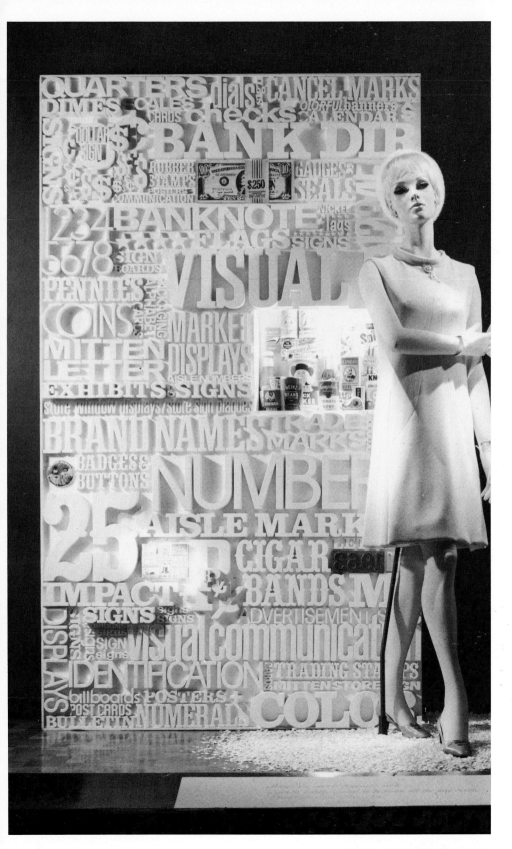

A few years ago Mitten's Designer Letters presented "A Christmas Studio" in their exhibit at the National Association of Display Industries show "Christmas week". We think you will enjoy reviewing the designs. They illustrate the variety of materials and ideas that are available to displayers. Write Mitten's, 85 Fifth Ave., New York 10003 for their free idea file, complete with style sheets and prices.

A Christmas cookie with asterisk decor.

A deep dimensional pine letter.

Square dots form the hat.

Another dimensional letter with gold leaf.

Christmas cards in shadow box form.

The head shape came from a scrap on the carpenter's floor.

A stylized tree and a Christmas trim bird.

Mitten's Vista lettering and U's form the border.

Capital C's and half-rounds form this border.

Three traditional pomanders.

A star shaped interlock.

Mitten's Executive on multi-colored felts.

A. A pine board sawed and varnished to simulate butterscotch.
B. The words Noel form a tree-shaped platform.
C. Felt covered Upson with embroidered trim.
D. A pair of authentic wooden shoes and the famous Dutch apples.
E. A huge rubber stamp using Montclair Standees.

The pyramid-shaped Ceppo, Italy's equivalent of a Christmas tree.

Two cubes for use anywhere: one with an old print and one with Mitten's petals.

A stylized snowflake with Mitten's Trade Winds on green plexiglass.

Stars and Montclair letters and numerals form this distinctive sign.

A simple design of stacked spools form a four-tiered tree.

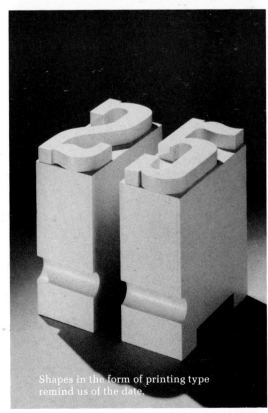

Shapes in the form of printing type remind us of the date.

Real barn board, metal decor and leather straps form an old country sign.

CHRISTMAS PUNCH

PAUL REVERE ★ SILVERSMITH

Stained walnut and spindles for a design to be used at Christmas time or for your Bi-Centennial promotion.

BOOKS for CHRISTMAS

An old print and Mitten's Show Boat letters.

HAVE A WHALE OF A CHRISTMAS

A standard whale sign and Mitten's letters.

A.

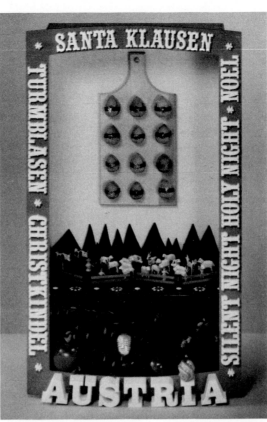

A. From the land of Charles Dickens comes the Yule Log and an old archive print.

B. An Austrian inspired display where the greens and apples signify hope. During the twelve days of Christmas a board is arranged with 12 nut shells, each filled with a tiny gift.

C. The Christmas Barn could be constructed from Upson and placed at the end of an entire floor of your store. It could feature greeting cards, wraps, small gifts and food baskets.

D. An old candle box, sleigh bells and a candy jar form a perfect backdrop for a small Christmas window.

C.

D.

A. Christmas caboose, a complete shop or a back wall treatment.

B. A Santa Jack-in-the-box.

C. A Scandinavian Christmas with all of the traditional forms.

D. Patterned after an old Pub sign.

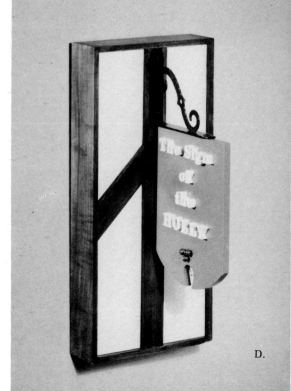

A. Christmas mobiles formed from Upson Easy Curve.

B. A Christmas candle interlock.

C. A happy Christmas shop idea.

D. Simple open fluted corrugated stock glued in circular and flat forms.

A.

B.

C.

D.

International Design Corp., 1147 W. Ohio St., Chicago 60622, has an interesting group of polyurethene Christmas cookie shapes, available in natural or sugar-coated finish. The Santa cookie is 17″ x 26″ and the Mexican bread design in the lower left hand corner is 15½″ high.

A beautiful box of things
for the Twelve Days of

We didn't have room to devote a full section to Decorative Spots but we thought you'd enjoy seeing the introductory page.

The multi-tiered toy display shelf could be constructed in the normal manner or it could be made as an interlock. The serpentine design can be achieved with a simple pine framing with outer surfaces of Pebbled Upson. The final finish could be one of many different types, felt, sand textured paint, contact papers, etc.

BOLT GLUE NAIL

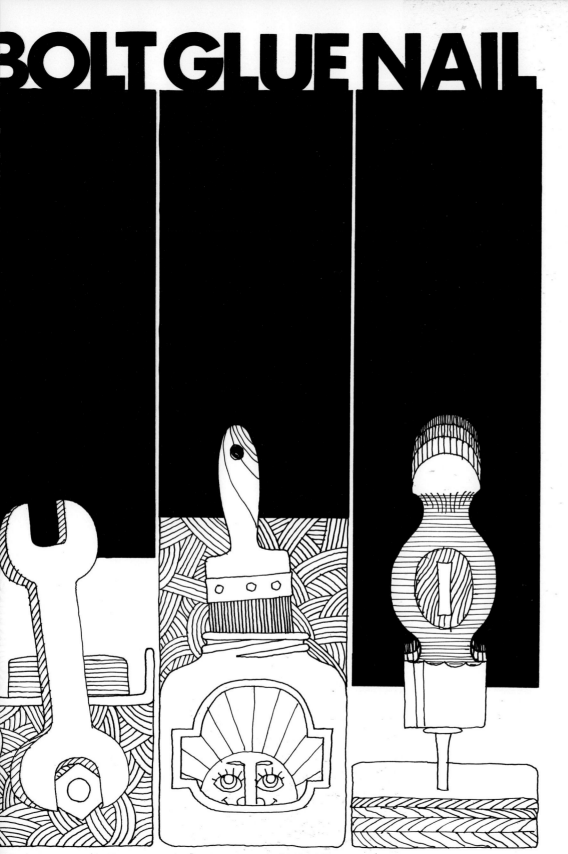

One of the only times that we have seen Upson actually bolted was in the erection of an exhibit, where thick exhibit walls were constructed and then jointed — exposing the washer and the nut. On page 278 we describe panelizing in general and on page 279 are four different styles of panel core construction. These are the types of thick panels we are describing when bolting is involved.

All kinds of white glues (synthetic resins) are ideally suited for gluing Upson panels, but we especially recommend the Slomons Laboratories glues for the best bonding. The chart on page 155 describbef the different kinds of glues that they offer and the materials that they bond.

The size of nails to be used in any project depends, of course, on the size of panel used and the holding power desired. Upson can be treated exactly like wood and the dimples caused by the hammer-head or any other nicks can be filled with Rock Hard water putty, which comes in powder form, or vinyl spackling compound, available in tubes or cans. When either one of these are hard a light sanding will bring a completely clear surface, which will readily accept paint.

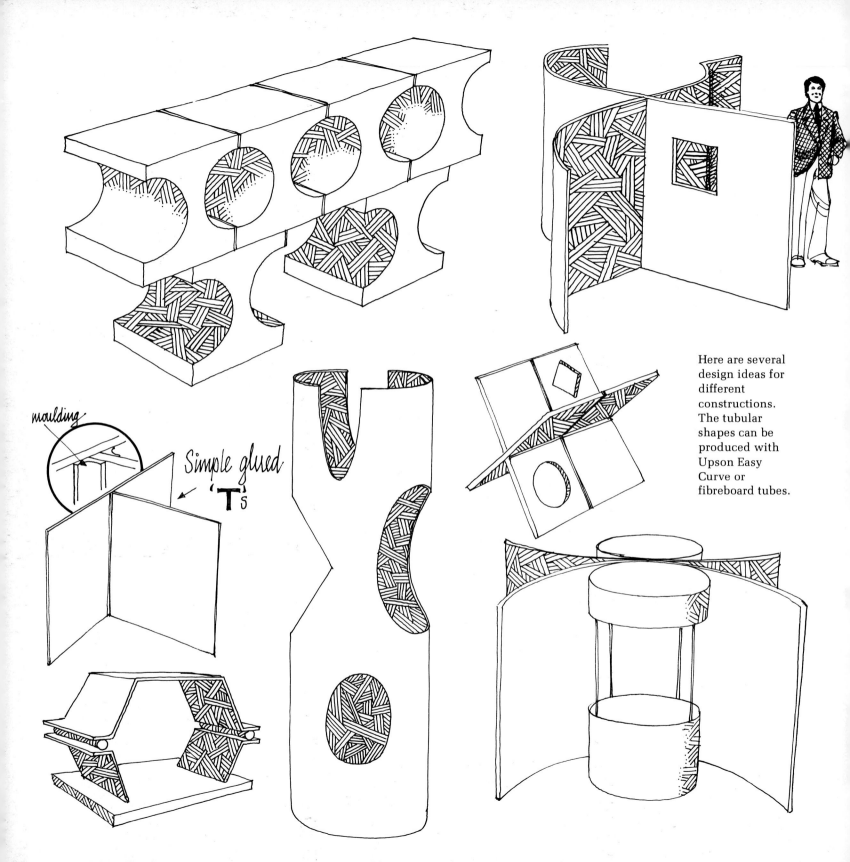

moulding

Simple glued 'T's

Here are several design ideas for different constructions. The tubular shapes can be produced with Upson Easy Curve or fibreboard tubes.

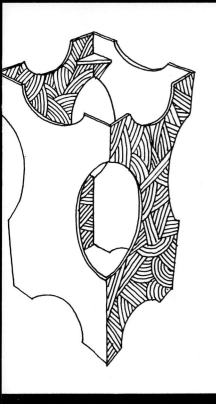

This stacked wooden form uses narrow wooden slats. Paul Hoppenfeld Display in Van Nuys, Calif., has used this treatment in all kinds of displays. They glue slats to a flexible base like canvas to allow for contouring.

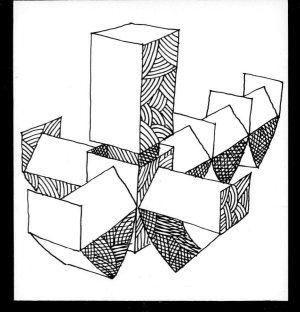

The see-through construction can be produced by cutting Upson forms and joining them in the corner with triangular shapes or wooden blocks. The form below uses the hexagram form, based on a polygon having three equal sides. It could be a hexahedron.

These two forms are suggestions for exhibits and displays.

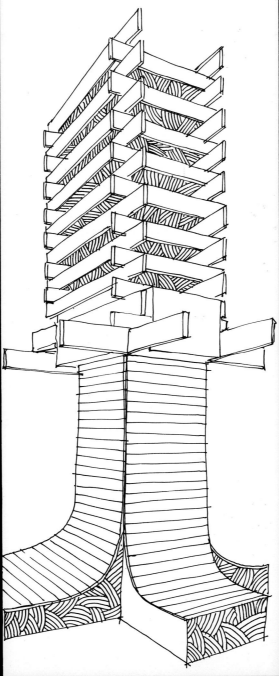

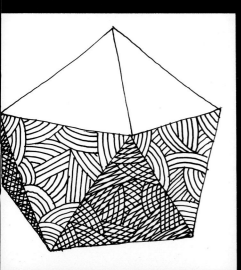

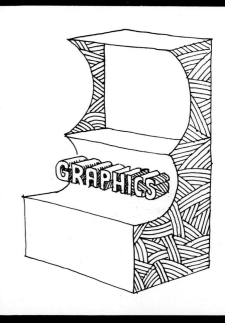

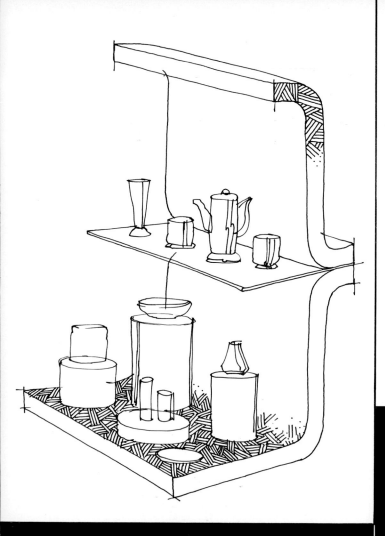

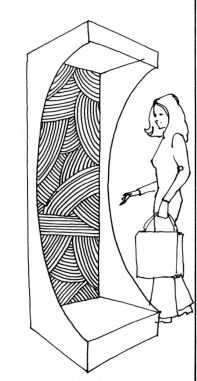

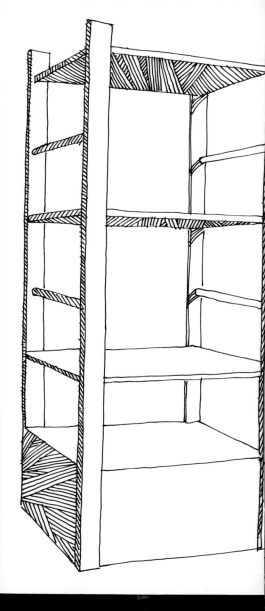

The form for this display was seen in the Museum of Contemporary Crafts show about paper. It was made from laminated corrugated utilizing a plexi-glas shelf. That same method can be duplicated here or Upson Easy Curve can be glued and nailed to wooden forms.

Here's a simple plain wooden shelf arrangement using pine dowels and natural wood following the trend, Mitten's or vinyl flat surface letters can be

Quite some time ago the Special Events Section of Macy's contacted us for large panels of Upson, to be used for serpentine walls in a special exhibit of Italian furnishings. Here we have shown a comparable idea — using this approach for one room.

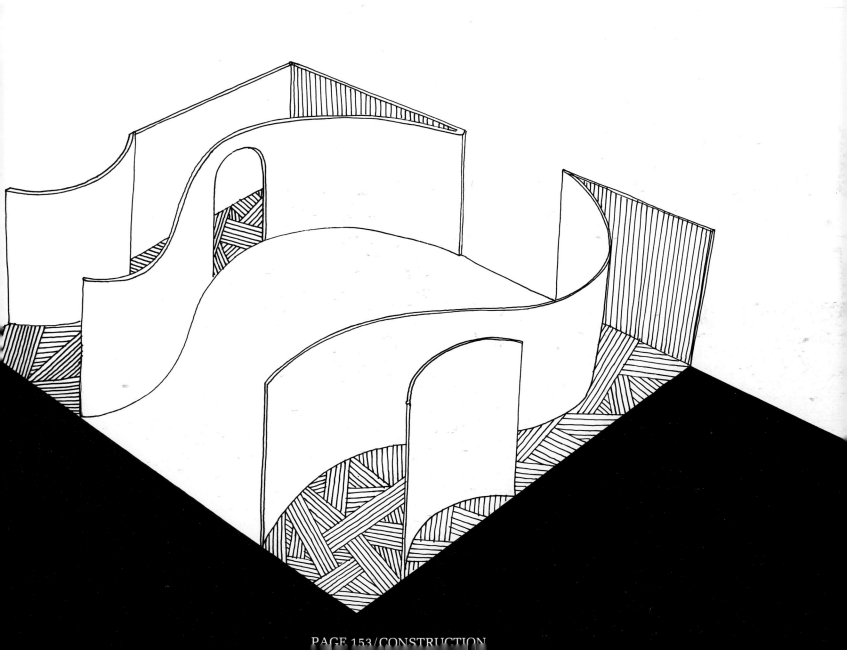

Two more ideas — 1 based on rectangular and square shaped panels and the other using triangular and rectangular shaped panels.

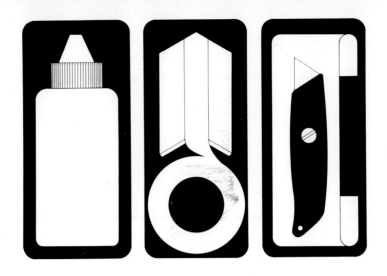

SLOMONS CRAFT GLUE PROJECT CHART

PROJECT	SOBO	VELVERETTE	QUIK
Draped Figures	●		
Decoupage	●		
Repousse		●	
Egg Carton Projects		●	●
Foil Projects to Porous			●
Burlap (resin impregnated)			●
Beaded Ornaments		●	
Plastic Flowers			●
Velvet Ribbon Flowers	●	●	
Fabric Trims	●	●	●
Plastic Trims			●
Paper Mache	●		
Macaroni		●	
Feathers		●	
Candle Trims	●	●	●
Art Foams		●	
Plastic Cup Projects			●
Glitter	●		
Sequins and Jewels	●	●	●
Styrofoam	●	●	●
Fabric Flowers	●	●	●
Cork and Upson Board	●	●	●
Collage	●		
Costumes	●		
Dried Floral Arrangements	●	●	
Seed Pictures	●	●	
Padding and Book Repair	●		
Glass and Wood	●		
Shoe Covering	●	●	
Straw Braid	●	●	●
Bridal Effects	●		
Vinyl Wall Covering			●

SLOMONS LABS INC.
32-45 HUNTERS POINT AVENUE,
LONG ISLAND CITY. NEW YORK 11101

GLUING —

Upson board glues beautifully with the white glues, as described on page 149. We are happy to recommend the Slomon's Laboratories three types of glues, which are ideal for use with Upson:

JOINT TREATMENT —

Because Upson products are made of wood fibers, they will tend to expand slightly if exposed to abnormally high moisture conditions. It would be wise to condition the panels prior to use, by permitting them to stabilize to the existing moisture conditions. Here are some typical joint treatments:

(a) leave a ⅛″ space between panels
(b) cover the opening with pine molding
(c) bevel the corners — leave ⅛″ space for expansion or contraction.
(d) if you use aluminum channel moldings, make sure you leave room for movement inside.
(e) pressure sensitive tapes can also be used.

SANDING —

Fine quality Upson fibers make it possible to sand all Upson edges as smooth as glass. A simple wood block with fine sandpaper will do the job.

CRAFTSMEN

Yarn-dyeing

Potters wheel

Potter at work

Quilt-making

Four-Shaft Loom

Spinning yarn

There cannot be complete understanding of crafts unless there is a comprehension of the human element in them and the conditions under which they grew.

No single term such as primitive, pioneer, natural, provential or self taught can label this important segment of our culture, here and around the world.

All of us have sensed a new interest and an intensified awareness of hand skills and we think a well organized crafts festival in your store could be a real traffic builder.

An example of a simple wooden toy

A total program can be organized involving many departments of your store. Naturally, the finished pieces will be on sale and the central vehicle in each area will be actual demonstrations. These could be set up in different departments, (glassware, gifts, housewares, etc.) and in some of your high traffic windows. The list of demonstration possibilities is endless. Wooden ware of all kinds, including toys, furniture, wood carving and kitchen utensils. Also basket weaving, leather crafts, glass blown, toy lead soldiers, cast and painted, ceramics, macrame and many more.

Other craftsmen can be sponsored by national manufacturers and include demonstrations on making high quality leather shoes and bags, jewelry, fine furniture carving, fabric weaving, etc.

These promotions can be local and regional in scope and generate not only a great deal of interest from the public, but also from the local media, including television and newspapers.

By contracting local art gallery shops and crafts societies you are sure to find many talented artists on which to base your promotion.

This gives you a good idea of how creative basket-weaving can be

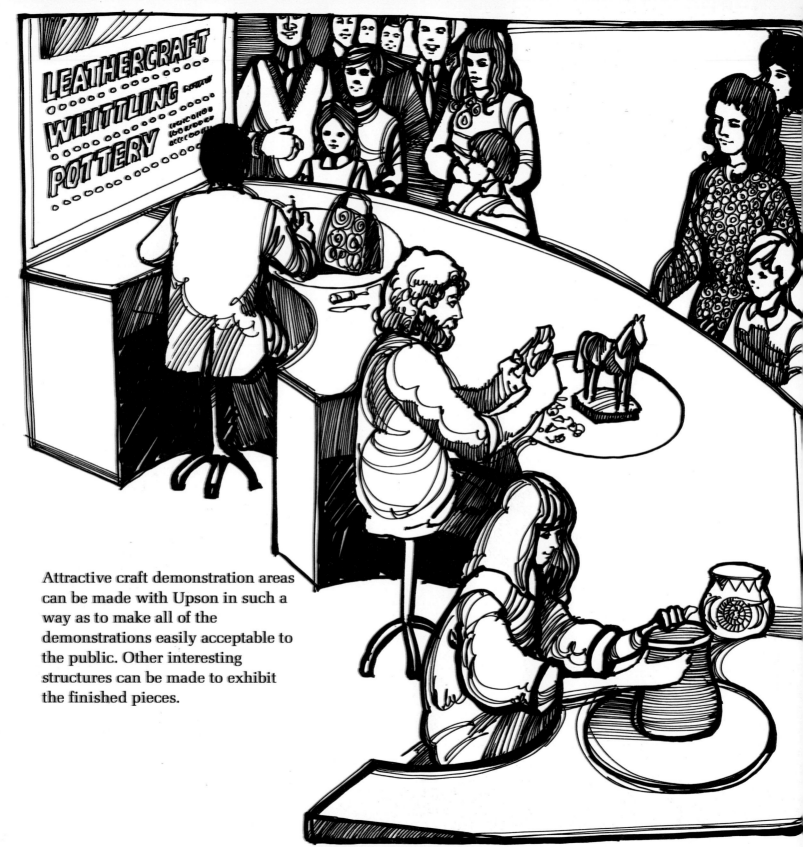

Attractive craft demonstration areas can be made with Upson in such a way as to make all of the demonstrations easily acceptable to the public. Other interesting structures can be made to exhibit the finished pieces.

On a recent trip to New York we stopped and photographed a fascinating demonstration of two young people cutting, sanding and assembling charming wooden toys in the front window of the Design Research showroom 53 East 53rd St.

It was a perfect example of real public interest and enthusiasm. It proves how fascinated people can be when they observe artists at work.

CITYFAIR

In the Summer of '73 the Hallmark Gallery in New York (now closed and converted to a sales area) created a fair on Fifth Avenue and called it "CITYFAIR".

The exhibit was in two parts. The first part was a formal display of historical records and memorabilia about the origin of fairs. The second section was the fair itself. Craftsmen were provided with booths made of barn board, burlap and swagging canopies, to give a rustic look. Hand made banners itemized each booth with the craft that was being demonstrated that day. There were eleven craft booths, a cashier booth/store and a small stage with two painted American folk scenes as backdrops for the participating entertainers. The entertainment included folk singers, mimes, puppeteers and Renaissance and folk musicians. Hallmark registered an attendance of 56,122 people.

aspenridge

In June of 1972, we visited the extremely beautiful Des Moines Art Center in Iowa. After making a slow tour of this exquisite gallery, we stopped in the gallery shop to look at the local craft items on sale that day. An amazing group of ceramic figures caught our eye. Here were Elizabethan queens and kings, a fantastic pair of characters from a German opera and a beautiful, yet comic figure of a school girl. We found that they were produced by Jo and David Hamilton of Aspenridge, Star Route, Laport, Minn. 56461. We have corresponded for almost two years now, keeping them posted on the progress of the book and they, in turn, letting us know how their careers were coming.

They are, as the photos indicated, two very talented people, who produce hand crafted stoneware in many forms. In one letter they reported the completion of 700 chicken-shaped roosters done entirely by hand drive which caused them to go "super weedy". Then they told us of some beautiful individual commissioned pieces similar to those shown here. They have quoted the following approximate prices and we feel that individual figures like these could be used in many ways. First, in your own home, secondly, as merchandise for your store and if you're in the advertising business, how fitting it would be to commission a custom piece for an advertising campaign.

(Approximate prices are: Seated or standing figure — $80.00 ea., Equestrian or flying figure — $100.00 ea., Figure in car, on motorcycle or bicycle — $125.00 each).

We realize that it might be difficult in handling some of these commissions by mail, but the idea certainly has potential. Don't overlook the fact that they are production hand-crafters, as well.

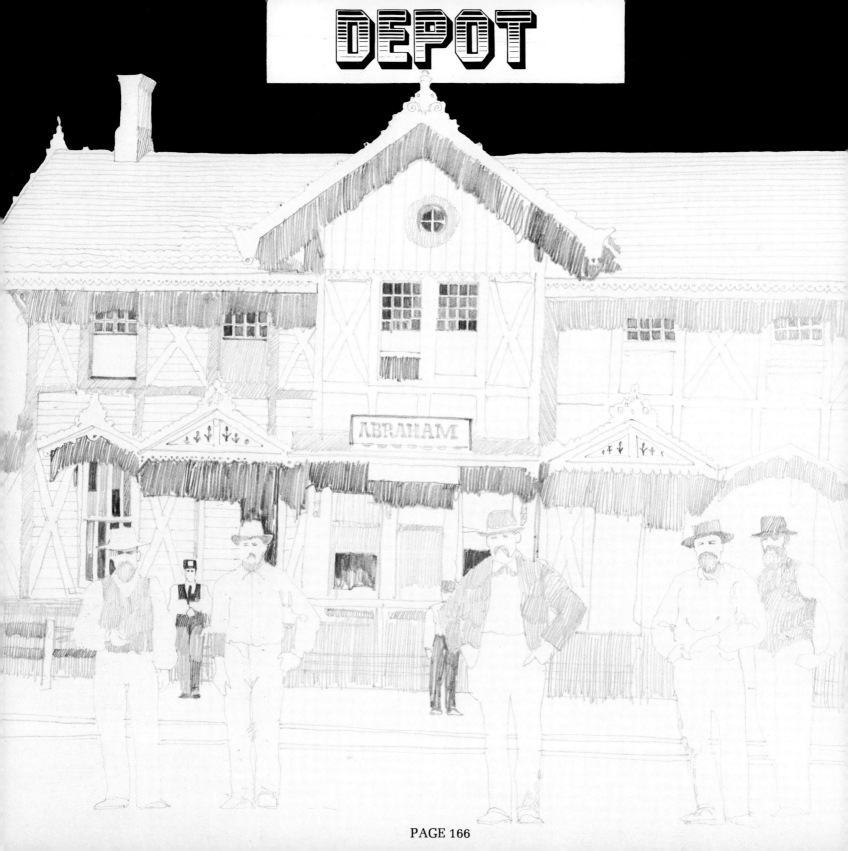

DEPOT

It will be hard to explain why we have a fascination for Depots, from a display and promotional viewpoint, we think they have a lot of potential. They combine so many things and express the feeling that a lot of people have for those nostalgic days of steam, sound and gingerbread structures. In practically every American town from the largest to the most obscure water stop, the rail station was a focus of activity and local pride. As a result the Nation became dotted with splended fanciful buildings and it is from these happy symbols that we have drawn our inspiration. From a merchandising standpoint you can construct all kinds of departments, symbols for windows and as shown on page 168, a complete area devoted to luggage.

USE BRIDGE DESIGN FOR A FREE-STANDING DISPLAY

Combining a huge print of a locomotive, the end of a building and an old baggage cart, we have conceived this idea for a luggage shop. The area in the foreground can be a simple frame on the floor, filled with polished river stones and the building itself can be made from different thicknesses of Upson board and painted in any of the rich bright colors that typified the western depots.

AN 1840 SIGNAL LAMP MAKES A GREAT DISPLAY UNIT

This elaborate lamp can be made completely from ¼" Pebbled Upson. It can be finished with brass paint with an occasional touch of green to give the patina that is found on lamps of this type or it can be covered with brass metallic paper or pressure sensitive stock.

The early 19th Century flagmen can be used throughout the store as your graphic symbol.

Many beautiful archive prints of depots and engines are available from Culver Prints in New York (See page 365) and we are showing several on these pages and on page 173. Please contact them for publishing fees on these prints. Other items come to mind that can be incorporated into your depot promotion. We think a richly decorated ticket window could be the central piece for your shop. Richly stained and varnished to resemble the well worn windows of the past.

Hayden-Trapani, Inc., 159 Second St., Huntington Station, New York 11746, produces a beautiful line of clock reproductions that they call "Clocks with a History". They range all the way from the famous long drop octagon regulator to the beautiful production of the Jolly Tar pastime advertising clock. They are, as you might assume, of the highest quality and the approximate retail cost of the advertisement clock is about $160.00. The long drop octagon is approximately $190.00.

Below a little depot sign made of Upson and incorporating Mitten's 3″ Montclair standees.

The gift shop in the Baltimore and Ohio Transportation Museum, Pratt and Poppleton Sts., Baltimore, Md. 21223, carries a full line of actual authentic railroad bells, switch and caboose lanterns, etc.

Write for their current catalog.

More
beautiful
Culver prints
and a classic
photograph,
The Old
Depot and
Hotel
combination.

DISPLAY SYSTEMS

There are countless systems available today and to show them all would require more pages than we could give to them. We tend to lean towards those that can employ ⅜″ or ¼″ thicknesses of Upson board (those that we have shown are also excellent for using glass, plexi-glass and other materials).

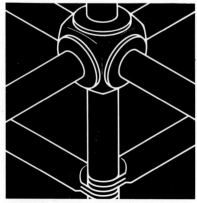

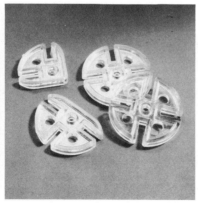

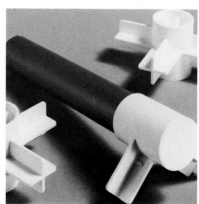

KEMCOR

The Kemcor System, 1235 Cedar Creek St., Racine, Wisc. 53402 employs three different types of plastic connectors, as shown in the lower left hand corner. Devised originally for use with glass, the connectors hold ¼″ Upson very nicely and all kinds of displays can be devised, using the three types of connectors. The table area shown in the second line sketch can be easily produced with squares, rectangles and circles of Upson.

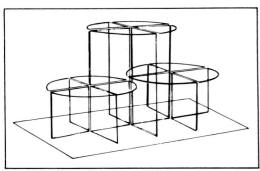

FOUR-WAY THREE-WAY TWO-WAY

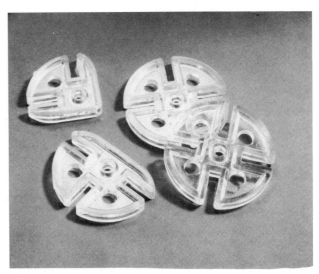

ABSTRACTA

Abstracta Structures, Inc., 101 Park Avenue, New York 10017. The principle of Abstracta is as simple as the system itself. It is conceived and developed as a lightweight structural system. Capable of maximum design possibilities with a minimum number of totally interchangeable parts. The key is the clever design of the connectors and the precision manufacturer of both tube and connector components.

We can't say enough about this fine system. It has extremely clean lines, uses Upson panels in dozens of ways and produces a modern structure that adapts to many display and exhibit situations.

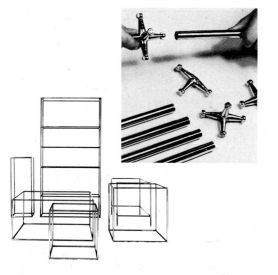

DEKO-BALL

We discovered Frans Beekwilder's Deko Ball System in an obscure little magazine and he was kind enough to send some samples of these unique little connectors. They are available in round and half round in silver and gray.

They are plastic and have small raised ridges inside of the slots, so that the paneling material is held firmly. We think the whole system is very versatile. Approximate U.S. prices for the Deko balls are as follows:

Large silver ball — 56¢ each
Half sphere   — 32¢ each
Mini Deko Balls — 21¢ each in Gray
                          46¢ each in silver

Direct all inquiries to: Mr. Frans Beekwilder, Prins Hendrikkade 19, Amsterdam-c, Holland.

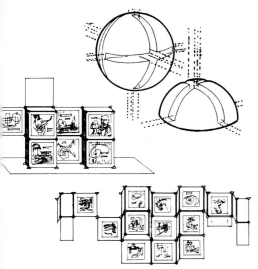

UNICUBE

This is a simple structural system, consisting of a universal corner connector, the "Unicube" and various lengths of ½" diameter round steel tubing. Individual and multiple structures are assembled, modified or taken apart in minutes.

The Unicube is made up of two mating die casting metal segments. They clamp the horizontal tubes firmly in place when the internally threaded vertical tubes are tightened. Custom finishes (gold, brass or consumer colors) can be furnished on short notice. Upson panels can be inserted with the use of shelf corner supports and vertical panel clips. Unicube Corp., 1290 Oak Point Avenue, Bronx, New York 10474.

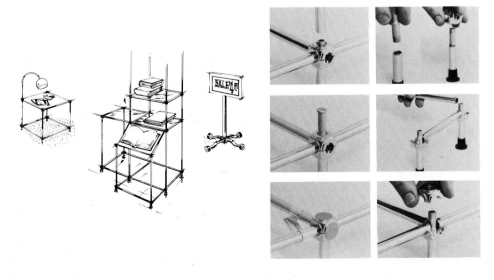

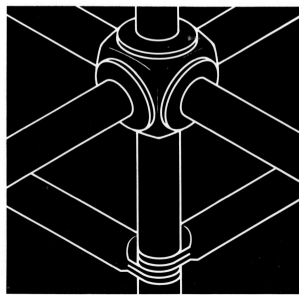

MOD-U-STRUTS

The pure simplicity and look attracted us to this inexpensive display system. It employs the use of 1⅝" diameter paper tubes and molded plastic connectors. The tubes themselves are available in light green, pink, yellow, white, black, red, orange and rust. Tube lengths are 12", 24", 36" and can be an effective way to show all kinds of merchandise.

Contact RTC Industries, Inc., 920 W. Cullerton St., Chicago, Ill. 60608.

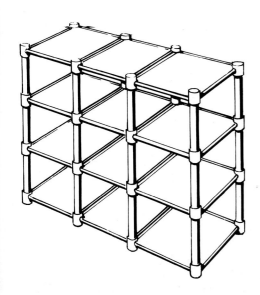

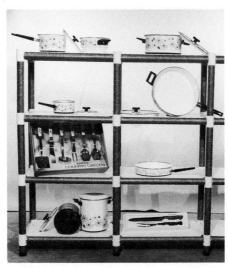

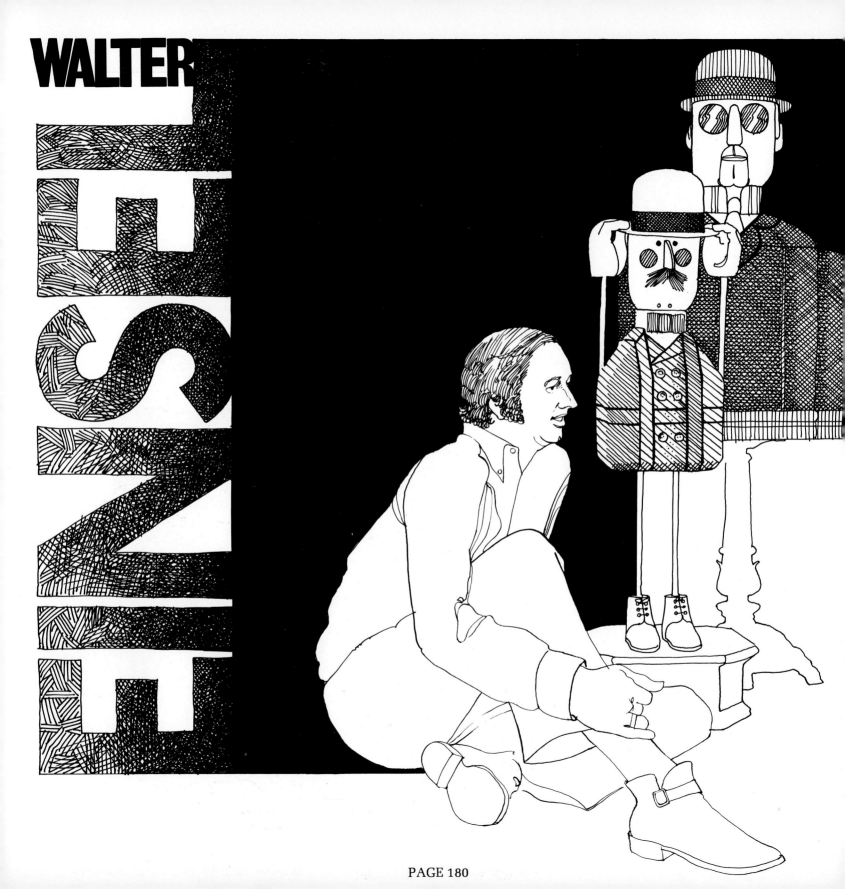

Walter Einsel is one of our favorite designer/illustrators and if you pursue magazines like Communication Arts, North Light, etc. you have seen his work. He was formerly an art director in the promotion department of NBC and in addition to being a skilled illustrator, his mechanical wooden sculptures have found an important place in American advertising art. The descriptions of the figures are in Walter's own words and they explain the reason for each assignment and how it was executed. He is married to another well known artist, Naiad Einsel, who has her own illustration assignments and collaborates with Walter on many of his large projects.

Walter Einsel, 26 Morningside Drive, South, Westport, Conn. 06880.

CAPTAIN MACY

This object was created for Macy's to be used in connection with a promotion celebrating the 115th Anniversary of the founding of the store. It is a representation of Captain Rowland H. Macy, the founder, mounted on a replica of the original store. It is over 4' tall and is run by electric motor. As the Captain slowly cranks his arms, the customers parade into the store. It was used in television commercials and then occupied a prime window of the store at Herald Square, New York City. A 14' replica was made by Macy's display department for use on the main floor.

This is the result of an assignment from ABC Pictures to create an image to be used in posters and ads to promote a film featuring Walter Matthau portraying a 72 year old grandfather. The bag of groceries and the park fence featured prominently in his portrayal. The most difficult aspects of the assignment were: 1. To capture a reasonable likeness of Matthau as a man 20 years older. 2. Produce the finish piece in four days. It is made primarily of basswood.

Built for Allied Van Lines for use in a television commercial, it is scaled 1″=1 foot and measures 27″ x 40″ high excluding the flagpole. It has 19 windows. There are 250 feet of pine clapboard, mitred individually by the builder. The corner posts are mahogany, the cornice trim is of oak. The window trim is maple, the chimney: cedar. The roof is copper, aged with vinegar, salt, a propane torch and five hours of anxious patience. I say anxious because in order to meet the television production deadline I was given 6 days to produce it. On the seventh day I rested. The interior rooms are decorated with old fashioned wrapping papers, the floors are stained and waxed. The back is open to be constructed in such a way as to allow them to slide away in order to allow the TV production crew a cut-away view. This added to the anxiety quotient to which I alluded. It contributed to a rather well-conceived institutional-type, soft-sell commercial.

A black and white photograph fails to give the impact of the pool-table green felt background which sets off the polished brass and copper of the various internal parts. The eyes, in the first position, are closed. Turning the handle, after a steel ball is placed in the mouth, causes the eyes to open and the mouth to smile. The ball drops into the brass funnel and down through the copper tubing to the staircase. As it bounces down the stairs, it makes the brass heart quiver and then drops into cylinder at one end of a balance. Its weight causes it to drop into the chute (at the same time making the sun rise). As it rolls down the chute, it hits a gate that makes the flag pop up and it ends its journey in an anchovy can. Raising the flag causes the parachutist to drop. The dimensions are 20″ x 48″.

This architectural study has a shadow-box style of frame and measures 17″ x 22″. The materials consist of birch, mahogany, oak (in the capital cornice), copper and brass. The sun and the moon are of polished copper and brass, the sky in the background is old rusted metal from an abandoned oil drum. The peaked roof frontices are cast iron. The dome is part of a float from a toilet tank (copper). The windows are of colored plexi-glas (orange and purple).

Reginald, or Excuse Me But you're Standing on My Foot. This figure stands 5′9″, is made of copper, brass, birch, oak, basswood (the head) and balsa wood (the hands, hat and right foot). When one steps on his left foot, he slowly dons his derby. Just as his hat goes on, his head rolls off his shoulder onto his arm and his leg kicks up. It all happens very quickly and most observers want to see it again. There is a ⅜″ steel plate under the oriental rug that gives the stability required.

Many years ago before radio and television there were hundreds of simple games to be played in the parlor and out of doors and there are interesting books written about the origin of games and their development. In our time we have seen Monopoly remain as the most famous game ever produced and as far as manipulation games are concerned the famous pin-ball machines absorbed many hours of our time. In this section we have tried to show a few ideas on how games and their shapes can be adapted to window display, signs and graphics.

GAMES

Many interesting forms
can be constructed to
make an interesting game
window.

Although it's been done before, giant Chess figures make interesting display units and the decorative pin-ball machine functions as a dispenser of games. Completely constructed of Upson on pine framing with spindle legs.

Decorative Pin Ball machine makes a suitable dispenser

FUN O GAMES

1,000

TILT BINGO

1.000

Giants

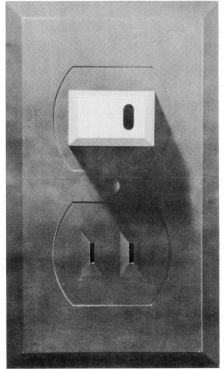

Throughout the book we have talked about giant forms and most importantly the size or scale of the units that you construct for your displays. Following that rule, any item shown in our book can be scaled either up or down. In this section we are showing items to be constructed in giant form.

The pure influence has come from one man — Claes Oldenburg. Born in Stockholm, Sweden, in 1929, he got his B.A. at Yale University, studied at the Art Institute in Chicago and stands today as one of the greats in the "Pop" art movement. On page 317, in the upper left hand corner, is a snapshot of his "Shoestring Potatoes" falling out of a bag and it exemplifies the beautiful sense of art, humor, fantasy and sensuousness that embodies all of his work. There are many beautiful volumes published about Claes Oldenburg and we have enjoyed every one. When you see his art, the first reaction is to smile, the second physical reaction is the urge to touch. His art is "Pop" and yet completely intellectual. This may seem to be far from the display field and yet it has been one of our favorite ideas in the projecting of one small item into a gigantic shape that speaks so much in conveying the feeling of the idea at hand. We have used this idea in many places, the giant bellows on page 31, super large paper carp on page 270 and 271 and in other sections . . . . Back-to-School, a giant pencil, Russian Easter — a giant egg, etc. and so when you come upon Oldenburg's giant hamburger, 52″ x 84″ made of sail cloth, stuffed with foam rubber and produced in 1962, you will be reminded of the theory of giant forms.

Expanding on the theme, a simple ice
cream sucker, huge box of pop corn and
peppermint stick.

Giants

For fashion promotions a giant magnet, a felt marker produced in giant form, with a ribbon banner and for office supplies — a giant paper clip.

THE MAGN

Colorful Fashion Fabrics

Giants

We are
indebted to the
Alling and Cory Co. of
Rochester, N.Y. for allowing us
to reproduce several items from their
"Tools of the Trade" campaign.
Giant X-acto knife; a linen
tester and an
inking pen.

Gingerbread

Victorian Architecture has long been in disfavor, however, we sense a renewed interest in the style and our reason for devoting a section of our book to it is that we feel the filigree and ornate detail, the shingling styles, pilasters, will lend a great deal of charm to your displays. A good example is demonstrated in our model for a Western store called "Tumbleweeds" shown on page 407. There are many excellent reference books on the subject. The Dover Publication, Early Illustrations and Views of American Architecture by Edmund V. Gillon, Jr. is a terrific reference guide to 19th Century architecture. All of the major architectural period styles are represented, Colonial, Federal, Greek Revival, Gothic Revival and Victorian "eclectic". The other book that we recommend is the Gingerbread Age by John Maass, published by Braham Hall House.

We are again happy to reproduce three of the interesting Mini-Mansion model kits produced by 101 Productions, 834 Mission St., San Francisco, Calif. 94103. These are three dimensional models printed in color on heavy paper, authentically rendered to scale by San Francisco architect Roy Killeen. They are excellent reference guides in architectural constructions in your store and besides, they're just plain fun to put together and look at.

In addition to the beautiful Art Center that we talked about in the Craftsmen section, Des Moines, Iowa has another beautiful landmark called, "The Hubbell House". The pictures shown here were originally Koda-color Instamatic prints, which we have converted to black and white. They do give you some idea of the richness of this spectacular house, located on one of the hills in Des Moines. The Hubbells were a prominent family in the 1890's and early 1900's. This is a classic example of the architecture of the time

Some additional reference. The photos on the right show interesting treatments for two gables and the depot photograph above is from Culver Prints in New York.

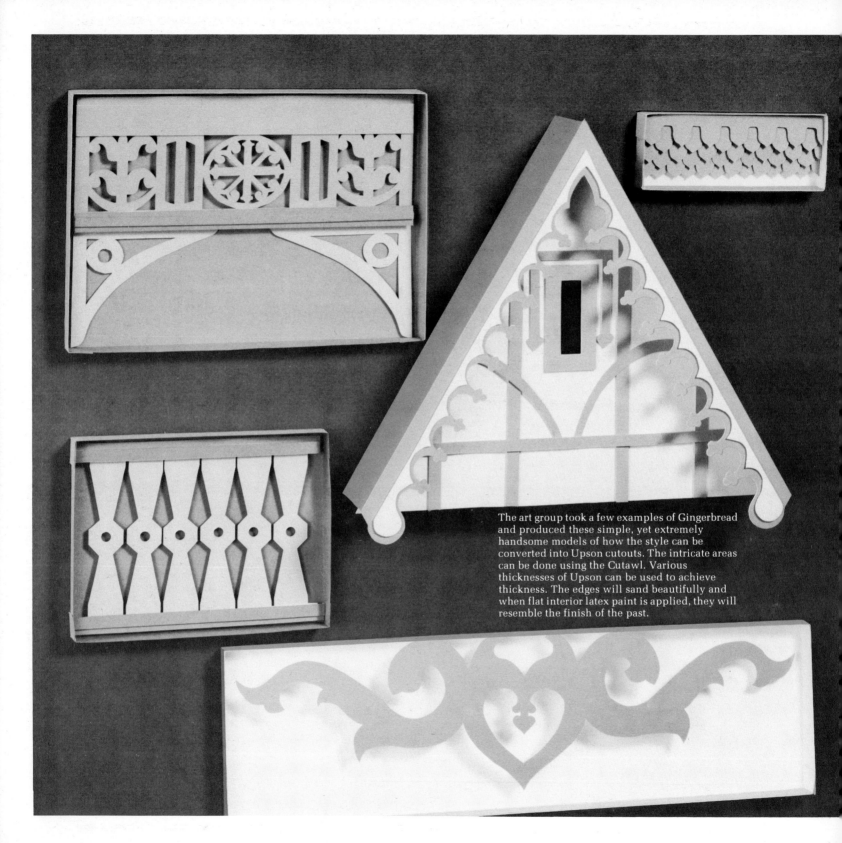

The art group took a few examples of Gingerbread and produced these simple, yet extremely handsome models of how the style can be converted into Upson cutouts. The intricate areas can be done using the Cutawl. Various thicknesses of Upson can be used to achieve thickness. The edges will sand beautifully and when flat interior latex paint is applied, they will resemble the finish of the past.

GOURMET

This section totalling 33 pages, covers many aspects of the subject. Basically there are housewares and kitchen crafts, constructions, five pages on meat, four pages on cheese and the balance is a potpourri of signs, suppliers and department ideas. With the growing interest in Gourmet cooking and the rising number of stores incorporating specialty shops, devoted to food, we think you will find this section extremely interesting.

Four ideas with a French touch. The cafe vignette incorporates old french entrance windows, a beautifully molded desert and classic detail along the top. Les Gros Bonnet is our design for a kitchen shop or a small restaurant within your store. The beautiful shape of the cork screw, cut from ¼″ Upson and mounted on a wall would make a dramatic symbol for your wine shop.

les gros bonnet

These two wall ideas incorporate the latest craze — natural wood. The bases for the Gallery Gourmet can all be formed from natural wood and the background panels made from Upson, each in a rich House and Garden color, velvet brown, orange peel, bitter sweet and chrome yellow. The kitchen craft wall idea utilizes big panels of Upson and food shapes stenciled on in stylized form or cutouts in dimensional form.

The housewares sign at the top can be handled in many different ways. It can be painted right on a wall pointing towards the department, it could be made into an actual sign using Mitten's Vista letters in 7″ size and underneath screw hooks could be mounted and actual kitchen utensils hung from them. The cubicle display shown at the right could be a see-through room divider on poles or an actual display shelf arrangement to hold merchandise. The food and utensil shapes can be painted on or cut from various thicknesses of Upson and mounted in bas-relief style.

Referring back to our Kitchen Kraft wall at the bottom of page 200, we offer some interesting design reference for use in painting your walls or for use as cutouts to be mounted on back-walls, entrances and on pillars.

·THE HOT STOVE·

FARM BREAD

Bread flour is a high-gluten ... gives excellent ... that is, if you ... well, (at least ... ...rry about ...neading

...en dough has ...ressing it dou... ...reheat oven ...ut 45 minut... ...ol on wire racks, away from drafts (which cau... it bread to shrink) *Eat and enjoy*

What kind of Gourmet Section would it be without the ornate stove? We have shown a beautiful one on page 23 in the Almanac Section and the Portland Stove Foundry page 43 carries many different styles. You might even be lucky enough to find one in an old junk store or antique shop. Placed on a low platform of rough hewn planks, your stove would make a dramatic conversation piece in the Housewares Department.

The sign incorporates some of the rich detail of these handsome old cast iron beauties.

Kitchen Kraft demonstration

This wall hitch-hikes on our big panel suggestion shown on page 200. It too, incorporates food and utensil shapes in large scale. Following our suggestion in the Craftsmen Section, it might be very helpful to have actual food demonstrations in your Gourmet Section and Housewares Department. It is a time tested way of drawing people into these areas.

USE A LINE OF GRATERS AS SHADES FOR LIGHTING A FOOD DISPLAY OR DEMONSTRATION AREA—

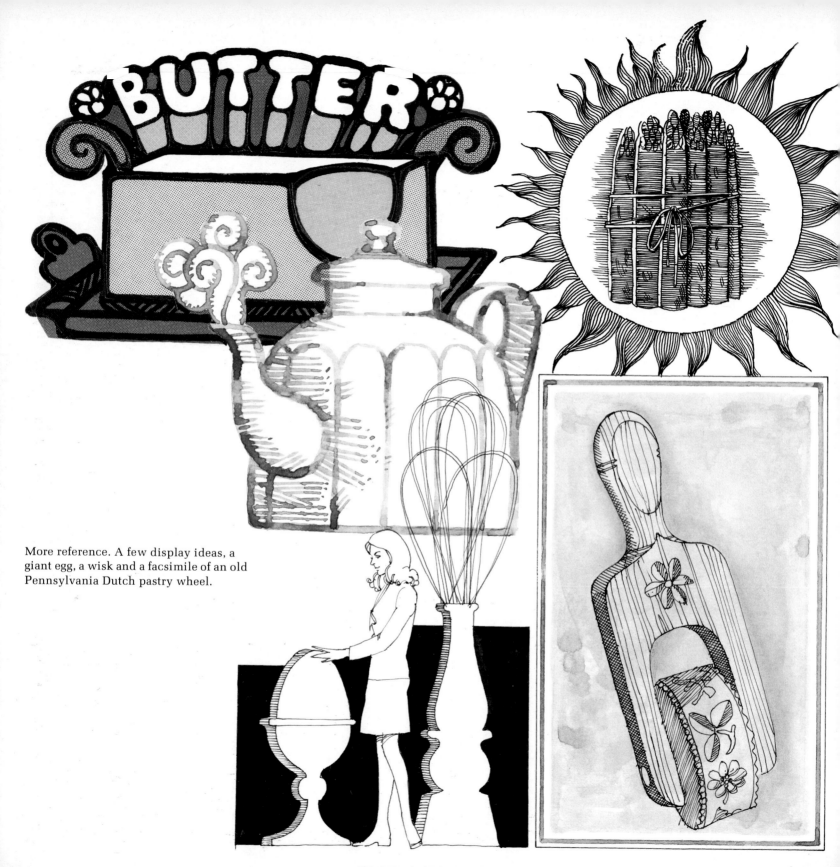

More reference. A few display ideas, a
giant egg, a wisk and a facsimile of an old
Pennsylvania Dutch pastry wheel.

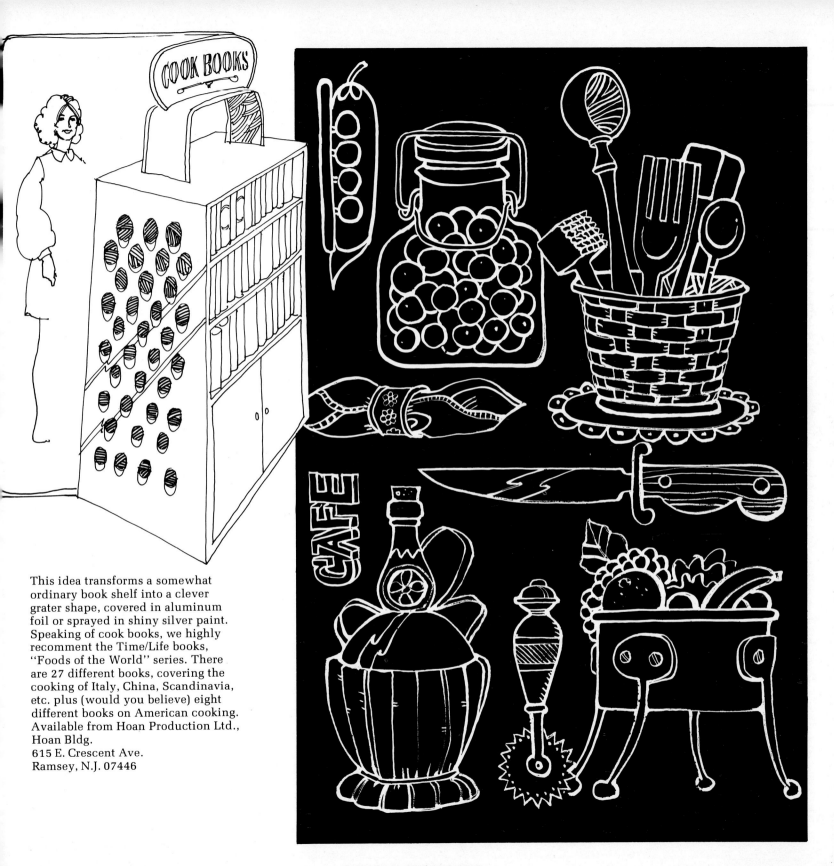

This idea transforms a somewhat ordinary book shelf into a clever grater shape, covered in aluminum foil or sprayed in shiny silver paint. Speaking of cook books, we highly recomment the Time/Life books, "Foods of the World" series. There are 27 different books, covering the cooking of Italy, China, Scandinavia, etc. plus (would you believe) eight different books on American cooking. Available from Hoan Production Ltd., Hoan Bldg.
615 E. Crescent Ave.
Ramsey, N.J. 07446

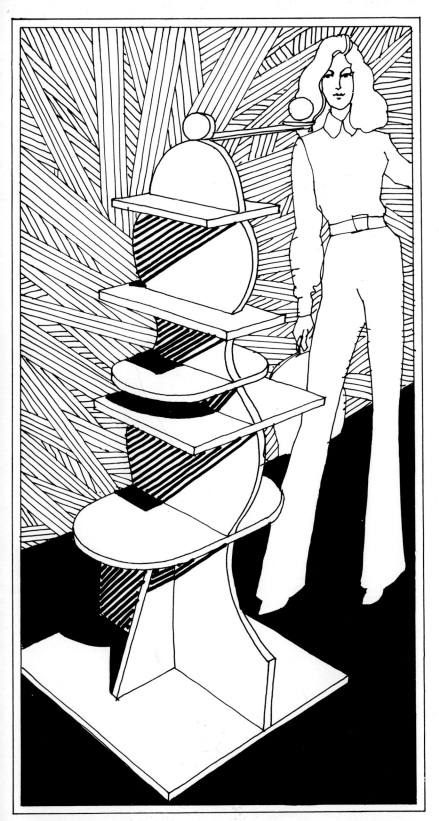

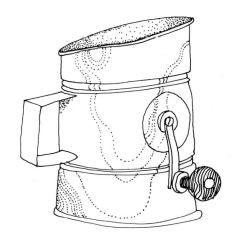

A giant peppermill constructed of walnut stained basswood or pine would make a perfect merchandiser for spices and condiments. Two brass balls at the top of the handle will add the final touch.

THE BUTCHER BLOCK

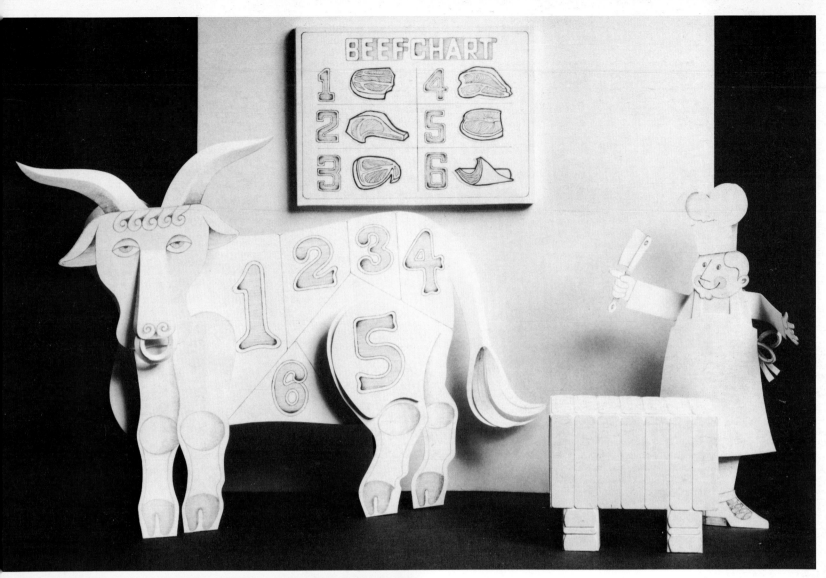

The forty-five degree angle of an actual butcher block has given us the design element for these ideas. Here is another excellent place to use natural wood as your paneling material. Slices of wooden dowel, stained slightly darker than the panel color will simulate the pegs found in real butcher blocks and combined with this could be smokey plexi-glas windows. Display counters and shelves could also simulate butcher blocks. Two major suppliers of actual butcher blocks, shelving, french baker's tables, etc. are J & D Brauner, Inc., 298 Bowery, New York 10012 and Butcher Block and More, The Schoenheit Co., 1600 S. Clinton St., Chicago, Ill. 60616.

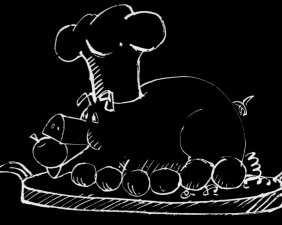

The three dimensional beef chart could be produced using Upson panels, Mitten's Letters and for a super realistic touch use some of the meat replicas available from Nasco as described on page 214.

Nasco, Ft. Atkinson, Wisc. 53538 are suppliers to the Home Economics market in schools across the country. We have been fascinated with their unusual meat and food replicas. They are used for teaching food preparation, but we think they could be effectively used in display. They are, as you might imagine, reusable. Approximate prices are as follows: The standing rib roast shown in the photograph is $31.50, the porterhouse steak is $10.75, the pineapple slices are $3.00 and the bacon shingle pack is $3.50.

It is just a wild idea, but some clever display man will put it to good use.

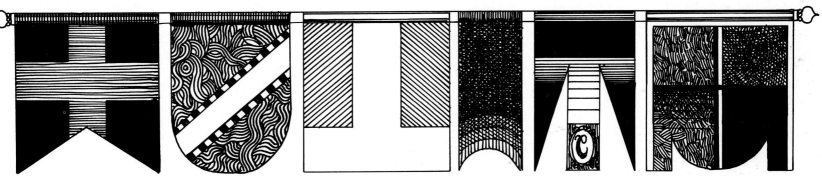

The cheese world is our suggestion for a shop within your store, selling cheeses from around the world. As our design motif we've shown the circular shape of a cheese wheel and it works nicely with the globe shape. The form is picked up in the door arches and to add a nice splash of color, flags of many nations either actual or produced in stylized form out of felt, to be hung throughout the shop.

THE CHEESE WHEEL

Our hanging sign is a triple thickness of Upson All Weather complete with Swiss Cheese holes and painted in rich satin finish latex paint. The old circular cheese boxes in the lower left can be reproduced or found in shipments of cheese coming into your shop. In the lower right hand corner on page 217, we have designed a simple cheese shop idea incorporating a natural wood ceiling device with the lumber notched like egg crating and supported by wooden posts coming up from the counters. Lengths of bright felt can be draped in a woven pattern from the ceiling. Emblems and the circular forms coming out from the sides continue the circular motif.

The Swiss Cheese and knife interlock could be made from ⅜ Pebbled Upson in giant form. And the old fashioned wrought iron rack could be cut from Upson and sprayed black with flat cheese shapes hanging from it.

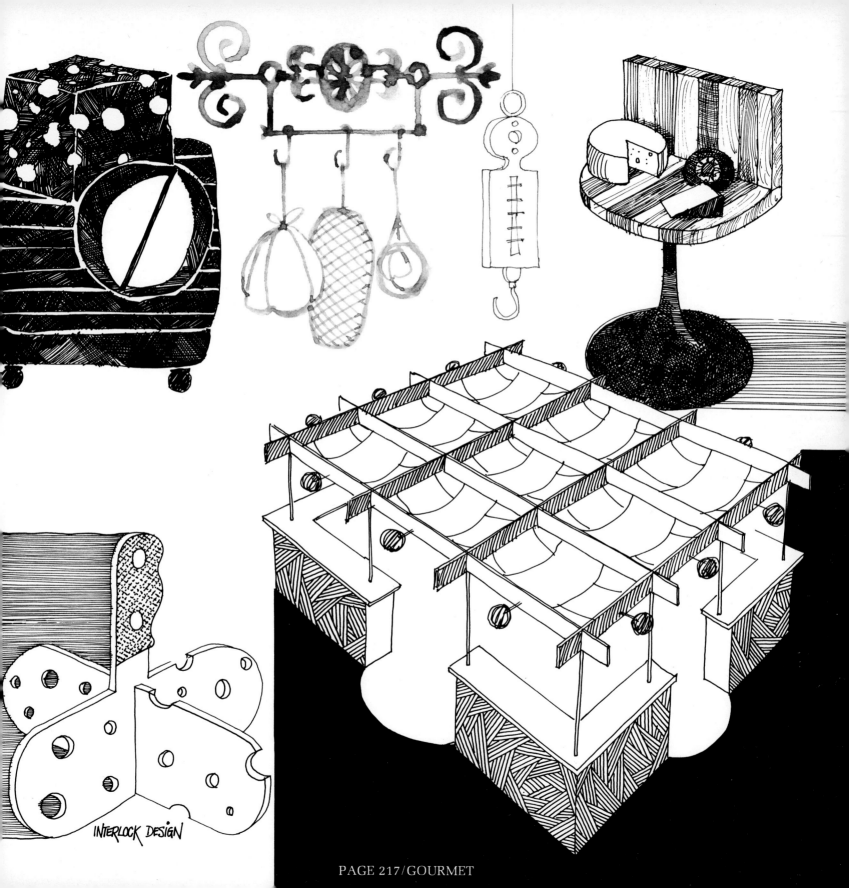

INTERLOCK DESIGN

The natural wood approach continues here with bold stencil letters, silk screened on the panels to simulate the packing case look. Our little chesse man stands on a giant gouda. The outside of this cheese shape is painted in shiny "wet look" lacquer to simulate the waxy coating. It can hang from the ceiling with a huge brass chain.

FRUITERIE

BEAUNE

Think how effective this entrance could be in the form of a huge coffee mill, decorated in many shades of brown and golds. The coffee bean shapes could be painted directly on to the wall panels or cut from ⅛″ Easy Curve, sprayed a rich coffee brown and mounted to add dimension to the wall.

Mushrooms, as we have shown you on page 223 come in all shapes and sizes and we have taken one form and stylized it to make this entrance idea. It can be used for a Gourmet Shop, a Houseware's Department or incorporated into an entrance for Teen fashions or a Children's shop.

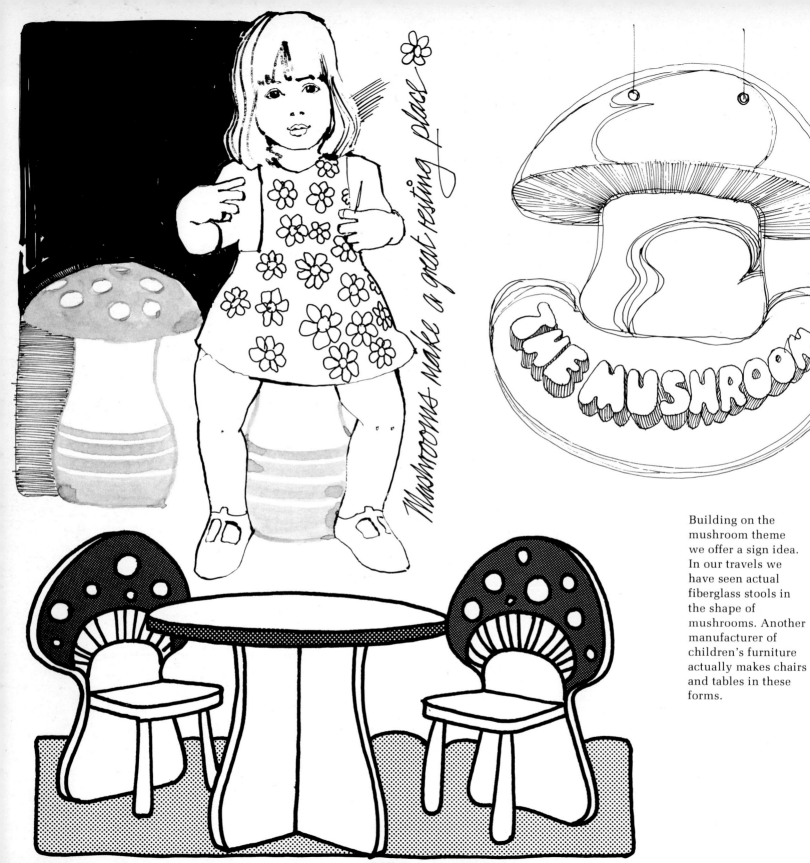

Mushrooms make a great resting place

THE MUSHROOM

Building on the mushroom theme we offer a sign idea. In our travels we have seen actual fiberglass stools in the shape of mushrooms. Another manufacturer of children's furniture actually makes chairs and tables in these forms.

Fruit shapes can take many forms. We've made a banana slide, an interlock apple, and pineapple and pear merchandisers. Fruit forms can be cut out for wall decor in many areas, not only those connected with food, but for use in fashion color promotions, watermelon pink, raspberry red, etc.

A quartet of food signs using Mitten's Letters.

PEASANT COOKING *OF MANY LANDS*

flavors of **HUNGARY**

recipes and memoirs by Charlotte Biro

Our good friends, Jacqueline and Roy Killeen, who produce the Mini-mansion kits mentioned on page 193 also design sell and distribute a very interesting group of cook books. Not only are they excellent in content as far as cooking is concerned, we think you would like to have many of them for reference.

Write 101 Products, 834 Mission St., San Francisco, Calif. 94103 for current titles and prices.

THE PORTABLE FEAST

vegetarian gourmet cookery

101 Secrets of Gourmet Chefs
Unusual Recipes from Great California Restaurants

THE WINE BIBBER'S BIBLE

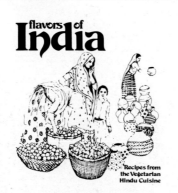

HERB cookery

flavors of **India**

Recipes from the Vegetarian Hindu Cuisine

MANNA FOODS OF THE FRONTIER

POTS & PANS etc.

Soup

MAMMY PLEASANT'S COOKBOOK

A Treasury of Gourmet Recipes From Victorian America

THE CALCULATING COOK
a gourmet cookbook for diabetics & dieters

hors d'oeuvre etc.

Throughout the book we mention the use of actual merchandise that can be incorporated into your display for windows. Tracy Dawson Imports Inc., 527 W. Seventh St., No. 205, Los Angeles, Calif. 90014 carries an amazing line of galvanized metal ware, wire baskets and Mexican tin molds. Write for the names of regional representatives and current prices.

Another excellent source of "Housewares of all Nations" is Hoan Products Ltd., Hoan Bldg. 615E. Crescent Ave., Ramsey, New Jersey, 07446. This unusual line of Gourmet cooking utensils covers a wide range of items. Copper bowls, omelet pans, whisks, wrought iron pot racks, steamers, porcelain pans and dishes, pepper mills, tins and other wooden items. Write for their recent catalog (wholesale only).

APRIL FOOLS DAY

Columbus day

FATHER'S DAY

POPPY DAY

Bastille Day

Easter

july 4

POW BANG POP

HALLOWEEN

LINCOLN'S BIRTHDAY

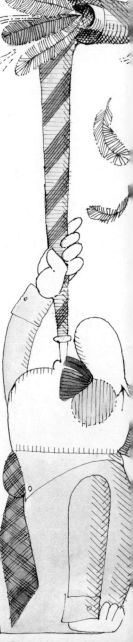

Contained on this two page spread are Holiday items to be constructed in any size. Decor and construction materials are up to you.

The July 4th design could be a deep dimension box or small window with the designs painted on the back surface of the glass or plexi-glas. Lincoln can be completely constructed of black felt 8' high on ⅜ Pebbled Upson to serve as a background piece for a Lincoln's Birthday promotion. We visualize the huge Election Day sale piece hanging from the ceiling on the main floor of your store, over a heavily trafficked aisle. It is, of course, a replica of the old style campaign badge. Felt and brass paint would be ideal for covering material. The turkey is in three dimensional form and we've also shown another on page 240. Happy Holidays!

We are indebted to Miss Margaret Martin of Buffalo, New York, whose original idea was to spread the words pattern to Easter out into a sun burst effect. We have hitch-hiked on this arrangement and have combined the typography with plexi-glas. Naturally, there are many ways to approach the construction. We suggest the entire display could be made from large sheets of plastic or the background piece could be Upson with the front part being glass or plexi-glas. Mitten's Letters in different styles could also be used, depending on the scale.

All of these ideas are self explanatory. The window idea incorporates Upson's Duo White 2 with the egg motif in the foreground and the tree shapes cut in duplicate form and stepped back, for a dimensional look.

MOTHER

GIVE MOTHER A BUNCH TOO!

Mothers love Candy

Mother with Love

Let your mother be queen for the day

This page offers all kinds of possibilities. We are especially intrigued with the beautifully designed tea cup and the slice of old fashioned hard candy, produced in sheet plastic, lighted from within to cause the candy to look transluscent, as though it was being held to the light.

The old fashioned line figure of the woman with the parasol would make a smart "theme piece" for your promotion.

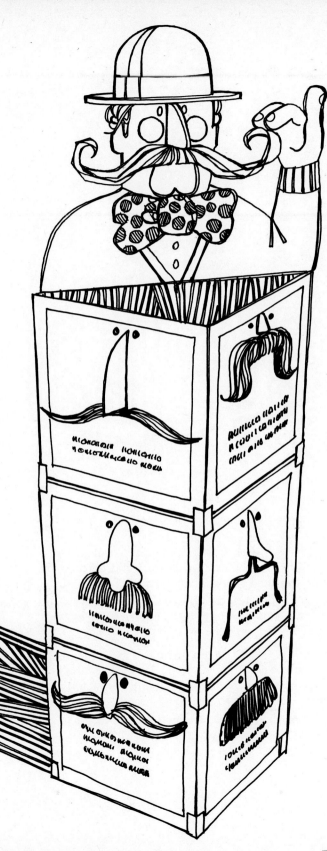

Would you believe an entire Father's Day promotion built around mustaches? Not only would you be able to make all kinds of clever window and pillar displays, using the mustache theme, but you could make a huge replica of the different shapes and hang them throughout the store, the tobacco counter, in the men's cologne department and an entire clothing shop could be converted into your "Father's Mustache".

Like the Centennial celebrations, held in cities and towns across the country, your store could sponsor a mustache contest, supported by newspaper and especially television promotion. Another thought is to have all of the men in the store sport their own or false mustaches, combined with straw hats, striped vests and garters on their sleeves.

Like the design shown in the Mother's Day promotion on page 235, you might want to make signs in the form of mustache cups from the old barber shops.

Two more background designs for Father's Day. We think the super size cigar could be a striking display unit or sign. The entire unit itself could be eight feet tall, formed with pine framing and ³⁄₁₆″ Upson board. The tobacco effect could be accomplished by using Kraft wrapping paper, ripped on some edges, clean on others, glued to the form at angles to resemble the way cigars are hand rolled.

The band should be very ornate, made from ⅛″ Upson with all kinds of scroll work, filigree with bright colors. Gold foil or contact paper will serve this purpose and should be used on the edge of the band and in some arrangements around the portrait. You may even blow up the pencil portrait on page 236 and insert it in the oval.

The watch idea has a nice modern look to it and the paisley vest reminds us of the turn of the century. The suspenders could be made from felt or giant ribbons through brass loops and touched off with real leather ends. If you wish to elaborate on the theme you could make ornate slides in the center section of the ribbon or felt.

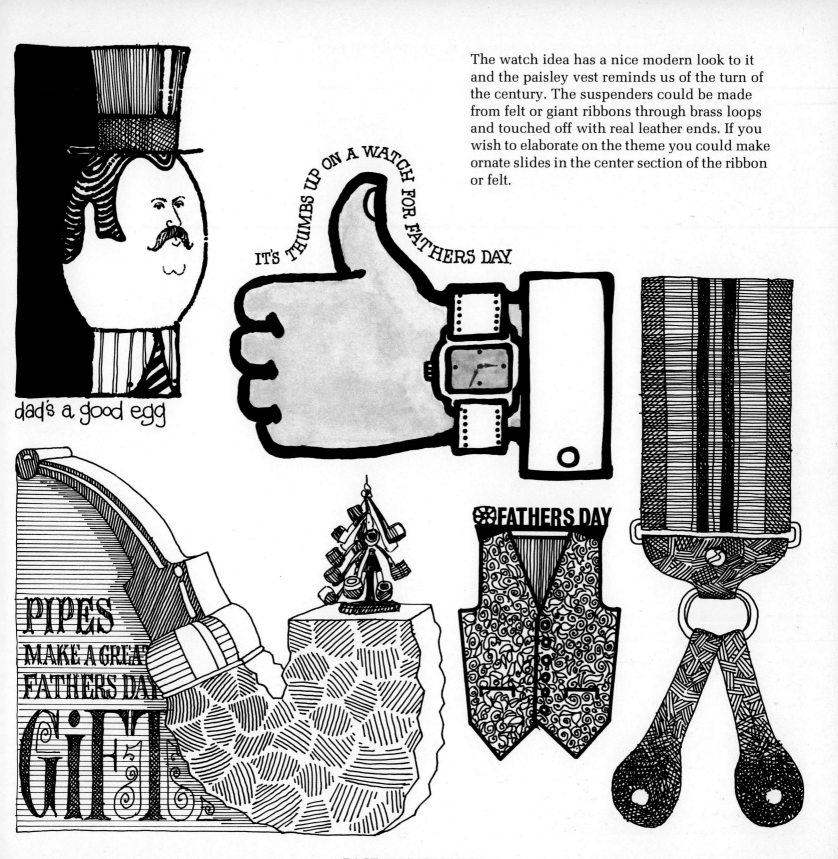

dad's a good egg

IT'S THUMBS UP ON A WATCH FOR FATHERS DAY

PIPES MAKE A GREAT FATHERS DAY GIFT

✻FATHERS DAY

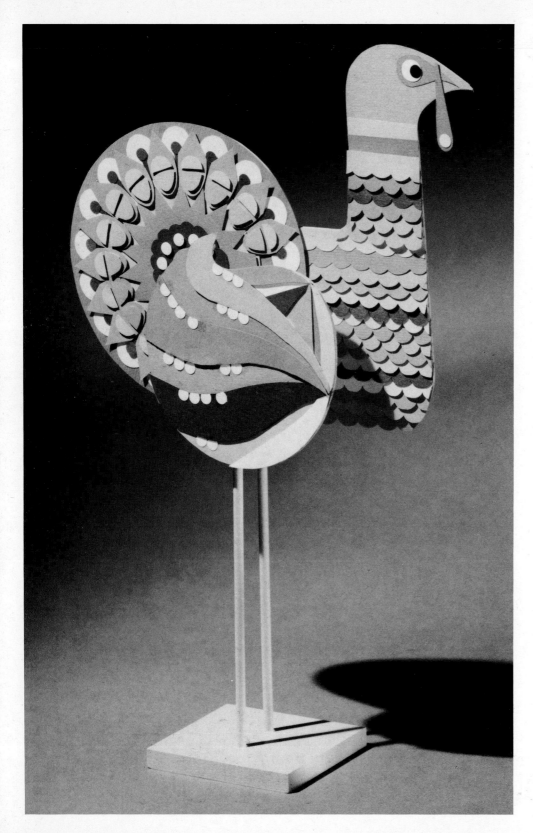

Our design group has
produced this charming
turkey that can be made
in all sizes. The forms
can be felt covered or
spray painted and the
legs can be large dowels.

KIDSWORLD

It is up and away with this youngster and the sign can be produced in several different ways. It can be completely flat, using materials or your own lettering and the balloons can be part of the sign or real ones, filled with helium.

THIS WAY TO KiDS FUNSHOP

HEY KIDS.

As a conversation piece in the Children's Department, a giant ice cream cone that doubles as a foot rule can be constructed and placed against a wall for occasional measuring. The disjointed jester could be cut from ⅜ Upson in as many separate pieces as shown and glued to a wall alongside the entrance of your Children's Department.

The harvest of tomorrow is the product of the seeds you plant today!

Simple forms in recognizable shapes are always an effective display idea. How many of us have built our own orange crate racers, played marbles in the school playground and have skated late into the evening until we were called in. This page would be most effective as a full background or individual items could be constructed for your children's wear promotion.

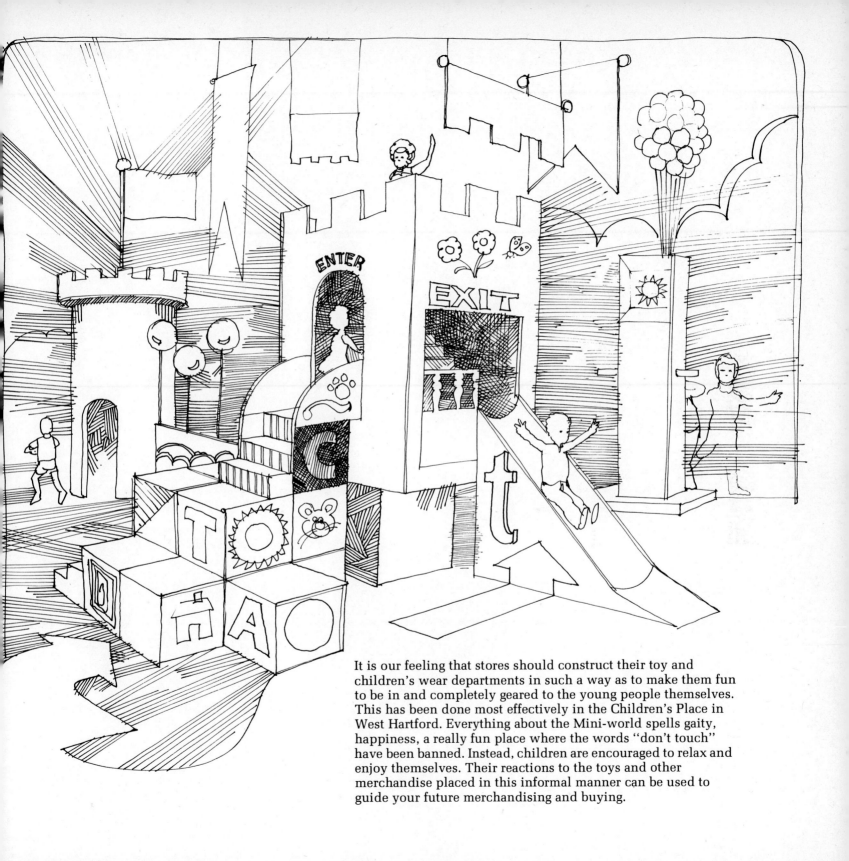

It is our feeling that stores should construct their toy and children's wear departments in such a way as to make them fun to be in and completely geared to the young people themselves. This has been done most effectively in the Children's Place in West Hartford. Everything about the Mini-world spells gaity, happiness, a really fun place where the words "don't touch" have been banned. Instead, children are encouraged to relax and enjoy themselves. Their reactions to the toys and other merchandise placed in this informal manner can be used to guide your future merchandising and buying.

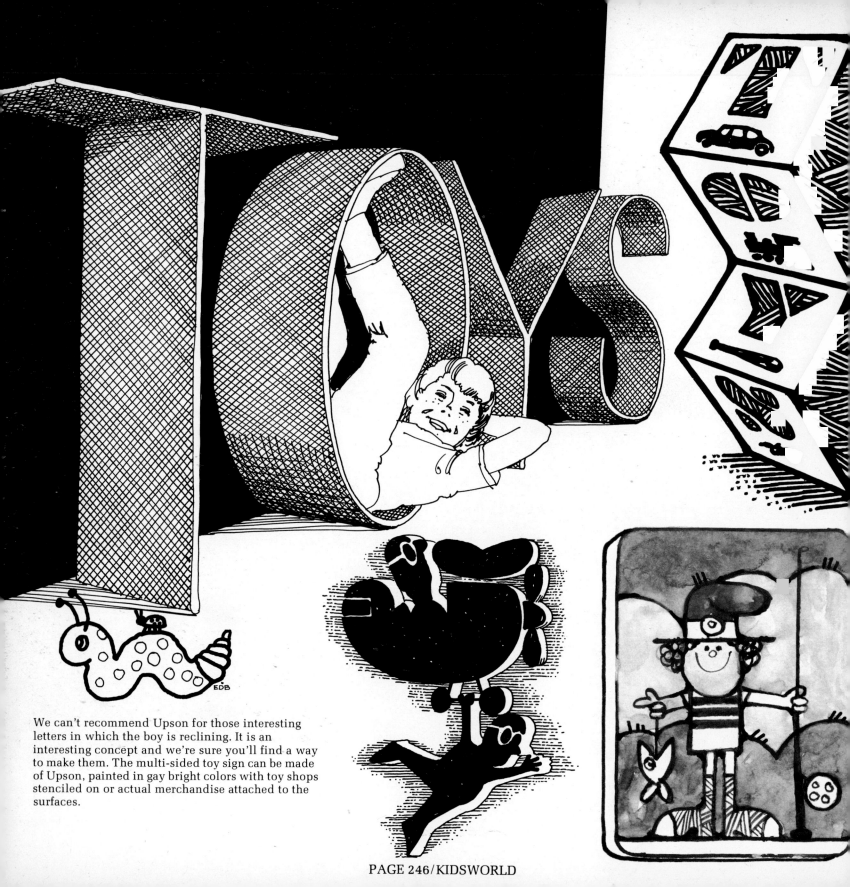

We can't recommend Upson for those interesting letters in which the boy is reclining. It is an interesting concept and we're sure you'll find a way to make them. The multi-sided toy sign can be made of Upson, painted in gay bright colors with toy shops stenciled on or actual merchandise attached to the surfaces.

Entrances have always fascinated us and this one could be a beauty. The ideal way to handle this one would be to carry those beautiful plush Steif animals, many of which come in actual sizes. We remember seeing most of these at F.A.O. Schwartz in New York.

WELCOME ABOARD

More animal shapes with lots of possibilities. The giraffe stairs could lead to a second level and the Penquin merchandiser is perfect for the children's department. The pig is a natural for Upson Easy Curve and different shades of shocking pink felt and a nice white yarn tail.

SWIM SUITS

PEEK A BOO

The Kidsworld sign was produced from a set of Creative Playthings blocks (Princeton, New Jersey 08540) and Mitten's Letters. The toy sign also uses Mitten's Baronet capitals on plexi-glas. The sign is especially unique as it has an open area between the two sheets of plexi-glas into which have been placed marbles and other miniature toys.

Bissonnette Play Kit, Inc., 1608 Barnum Ave., Stratford, Conn. 06497 produces this handsome General Store. It is a well designed, sturdilly made kit that retails for $59.95. We think it is a natural as a "play item" in your children's department. It comes complete with furnishings, hardwood roof and base.

An absolute zoo of animal merchandisers.

More animals and more fun. The big bird could be made from dowels, styrafoam balls and real feathers.

kiddies korner

A composite of all of the things we have
described in the previous pages are here. The
merchandisers and the entrances and the
sense of gaiety form a selling atmosphere.

"TO SEE WHAT EVERYONE HAS SEEN AND THINK WHAT NO ONE HAS THOUGHT"

It may not be a true analogy to relate what the Ontario Science Centre is trying to accomplish and what we were talking about on page 245. The Science Centre is designed to communicate in many ways, but its dominant element is the participation exhibit. It is a new environment, a playground for the intellect, a fantastic experience for everyone. Its three striking buildings at 770 Don Mills Road, Toronto, Ontario, encompass a world of discovery and fun. On the next two pages we have shown 72 illustrations of a few of the attractions. Participation leads to fascination and fun.

A spectacular diorama of a Canadian engineering achievement —the **spiral tunnels** of the C.P.R.

Come in, sit down and make music in the **organ room.**

The sectioned quarry engine, **Gertrude,** depicts all the basic elements of steam locomotive design.

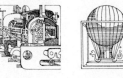

An operating **hot air balloon.**

Canadair's **VTOL** takes off or lands vertically, hovers, or flies normally.

This 1867 **steam buggy** may well have been Canada's first automobile.

The history of aviation is illustrated in an array of **aircraft models.**

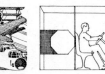

Test your **driving reactions.**

The **Islander** was a victim of one of Canada's first maritime disasters.

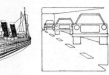

How good is your **judgment of distance?**

Find out what **gears** do by turning them yourself.

The **binary counter** shows how ordinary numbers are converted to computer numbers.

The **midnight sun** of the Canadian Arctic.

A wide-angle diorama of the **tundra** with its animal life, winter and summer.

An exhibit to let you understand **centripetal** and **centrifugal** forces.

A working model of the **Tokaido Express,** the world's fastest and most completely automated passenger train.

A **cable matching game** played with modern telephone cable.

A diorama of an ancient castle showing how many persons had to expend **energy** which we now command at the flick of a switch.

Revolving trapezoid makes you believe a suspended stick rotates through a window frame.

African kalimbas are mounted so you can play tunes on these primitive pianos.

Water pressure demonstration. It's the height not the diameter of the vessel containing water.

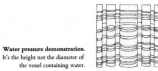

Pedal your way to making music, lighting lights and putting yourself on TV with the **bicycle generators.**

Star tracing unit demonstrates the difficulty of hand movement when viewing through a mirror.

The **light piston** is an optical illusion showing how intensity of light affects judgment in distance.

A revealing visual demonstration of the **Pythagorean theorem.**

Have your sense of relative size destroyed in the **distorted room.**

Ever hear you own voice delayed 1/10th of a second? The **audio delay unit** puts you in that situation.

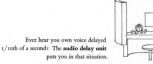

Create your own lighting effects from a professional console and see the result in the **theatre stage.**

The inheritence of **eye, hair and skin colour** is explained.

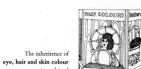

The nutrition of a plant can be controlled to produce a dwarf. This is the Japanese art of **Bonsai.**

Twenty varieties of live budgerigars in a huge flight cage illustrate **genetic variation** in a single species.

The **pituitary** is the master gland in the body and this exhibit helps explain why.

Priestley's experiment duplicated shows that a plant and animal can sustain each other's metabolism in a sealed environment.

 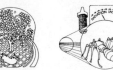

The **ant colony** is used to demonstrate the use of radioisotopes in tracing animal movement.

The **mineral requirements** of plants are demonstrated by means of living plants growing in cylinders.

The effects of the sex hormones on the development of a rooster are shown in the **capon** exhibit.

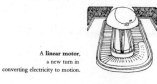

A **linear motor**, a new turn in converting electricity to motion.

Millions of volts from a **Van der Graaff generator,** earliest of the atom smashers.

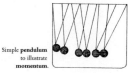

Investigate some of the basic elements of electricity and magnetism with the exhibits on the **electricity wall.**

An exhibit to help you understand the **stroboscopic effect.**

Simple **pendulum** to illustrate **momentum.**

A fantastic **tower** held together by modern **adhesives.**

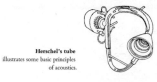

Is your **colour matching** ability as good as you imagine?

The **laws of probability** are illustrated in an exhibit which uses coloured liquid to create a normal distribution curve.

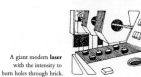

A dimensional look at the **mean annual rainfall** in 69 Canadian locations.

A colourful **relief map** of the **Great Lakes.**

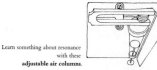

Herschel's tube illustrates some basic principles of acoustics.

A tiny theatre devoted to films on **animal behaviour.**

A giant modern **laser** with the intensity to burn holes through brick.

A multi-stage fractional **distillation column.**

Learn something about resonance with these **adjustable air columns.**

Investigate **what happens in a vacuum** with this group of exhibits.

Sorting ball bearings by size, mechanically.

One of the world's first operating **electron microscopes,** built at the University of Toronto.

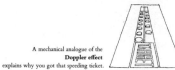

Stand in the light and create **coloured shadows.**

Learn something of the **interaction of colours.**

An exhibit showing the condition of **Acromegaly**–excess pituitary growth hormone– and how it can be treated.

Remote mechanical hands for manipulating radioactive materials.

A mechanical analogue of the **Doppler effect** explains why you got that speeding ticket.

You've heard your own voice – **now you can see it!**

What are the relative levels and depths of the Great Lakes? The **Great Lakes section** shows you.

Touch of luxury! The **Canadian furs** exhibit allows you to feel the difference.

Detecting flaws with the **Magnaflux technique.**

The **windmill** was the earliest machine to use a feedback control system.

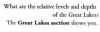

A large, accurately scaled diorama of the **Eisenhower-Snell lock complex** in the St. Lawrence Seaway.

The **hydroponic** exhibit shows plants growing in nutrient solutions rather than soil.

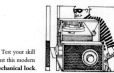

A model of the world's first **jet reaction engine** built by Heron of ancient Alexandria.

A reproduction of the laboratory in which **Banting and Best** discovered insulin.

A 50-foot map of the entire **St. Lawrence Seaway** presented on illuminated glass panels.

Cathode rays bent by a **magnet** to help illustrate the principle of the electron microscope.

Test your skill against this modern **mechanical lock.**

Three generations of **guinea pigs** illustrate the basic rules of **inheritance.**

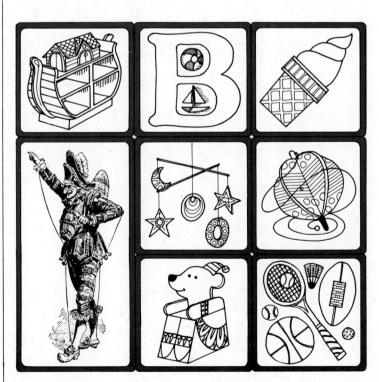

LONDONDERRY

The number of pages that we have devoted to Londonderry has only scratched the surface of this powerful retail promotion. The theme, like all other country themes can be used throughout the store. For starters you might want to follow the idea of exterior decoration, like the colonial street scene in the Bi-Centennial Section on pages 96 & 97 and the Vikingsholm facade, on pages 398 and 399.

Windows could be decorated to have a "leaded" look. The street scene replicas could be done in many styles, including the timber walling style shown on page 259 opposite and the thatched effect also shown on that page.

A picturesque feature of English medieval towns was the projection of upper storeys, one above the other over narrow streets. You can accomplish this on a small scale by referring to line drawings on page 262 and 263.

As we have indicated with our other promotional suggestions, it's wise to extend the graphics and style of the theme throughout the store including every conceivable department.

A natural, of course, will be a full promotion for the Men's Department. This can be carried through to gifts, with a special display of English china, pewter tankards and English Leather Cologne. An authentic tobacco shop and a restaurant might tie in with your theme, for added promotional impact! impact!

"The Granary" — instore construction suitable for promoting health and farm products —

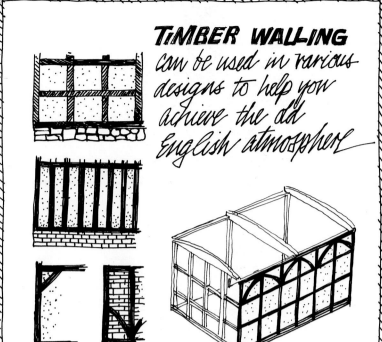

TIMBER WALLING

can be used in various designs to help you achieve the old English atmosphere

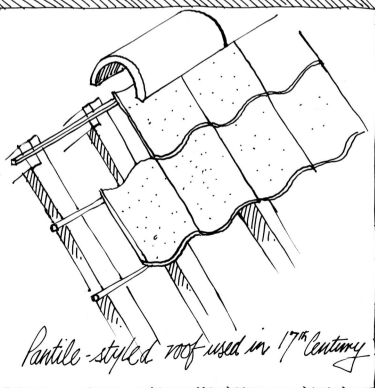

Pantile-styled roof used in 17ᵗʰ Century

Thatching — very English

I SAY, HOW AWFULLY BRITISH

TOP HAT MENS SHOPPE

LONDON

The elaborate Pub sign can be constructed using narrow gauge wire, wooden framing and a pole, plus a nice piece of pebbled Upson, painted in a rich maroon color. You might want to contact a local wire former and ask him to produce as many of this design as needed for use in your store-wide promotion. They might become your central graphic form and can be used in other areas including your window displays.

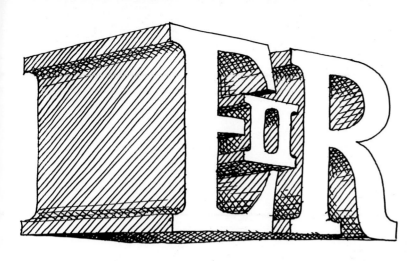

On the left we have suggested a huge deep dimensional form based on the initials of Elizabeth Regina, which could be used in your windows. The cricket sign is similar to the hand painted tavern signs in current use today.

A suitable facade for a Mens haberdashery

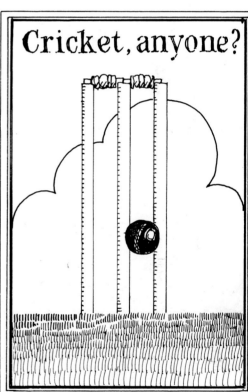

Cricket, anyone?

1785

The 12 line drawings shown on these two pages have been furnished to us by Arthur Barker Ltd., 11 St. John's Hill, London, England from their book "British Architecture through the Ages" by Leonora & Walter Ison. It supports the feeling we have that research is one of the most important tools of the display man's trade and when you are starting your promotion, it is always helpful to be able to work from authentic reference, so that your promotion has a rich authentic look to it.

Please do not reproduce these two pages in any form as the permission was given to us for *Upson Company use only* as a service to you, the reader.

Mayflower Marketing of Topsfield Parade, London, N8, 8 PR, England has furnished us with a copy of their model of the Tower of London. It is one of their series of book/records and models that we saw at the New York premium show. The two book records that we have seen are the Changing of the Guard and The London Pub, both extremely interesting and loaded with authentic drawings, photographs, and sounds as provided by the records. The photo on the right is a part of a spectacular Christmas promotion conducted by Dayton Company, Minneapolis, Minn. It used over **90,000** square feet of ³/₁₆″ Pebbled Upson board.

British Fare — a small selling area.

Mitten's Letters and the Union Jack.

A gigantic entrance idea.

A full shop idea on the Muffin's theme.

On page 378 and 379 we described Gargoyles Ltd., 512 South Third St., Philadelphia, Penna. 19147. These two pages have been placed in the Londonderry Section because the items shown have been produced in England and because they are so appropriate to this promotion. A full catalog of all of Gargoyles offerings is available for $4.00. The five Pub Mirrors shown are typical of a wide selection offered by this firm. Here is a quote from their catalog. "These mirrors were used by the English breweries as a form of advertising in days gone by. They have since become available collector's items and are widely used in restaurant decor. We are fortunate enough to reactivate the sources of this noble art, and are proud to present a product that equals, if not surpasses the qualities of its original predecessor".

Net prices (and these are approximate) range from $90.00 to $350.00 each. Please ask for current prices when purchasing The Gargoyles catalog.

Gargoyles also carries a very interesting selection of hand carved and hand painted wooden signs, many of them are in the Distillery category, but many others advertise tobacco, railroads, etc. Approximate cost for the Flor de Tobacos is $290.00 list.

ORIENT EXPRESS

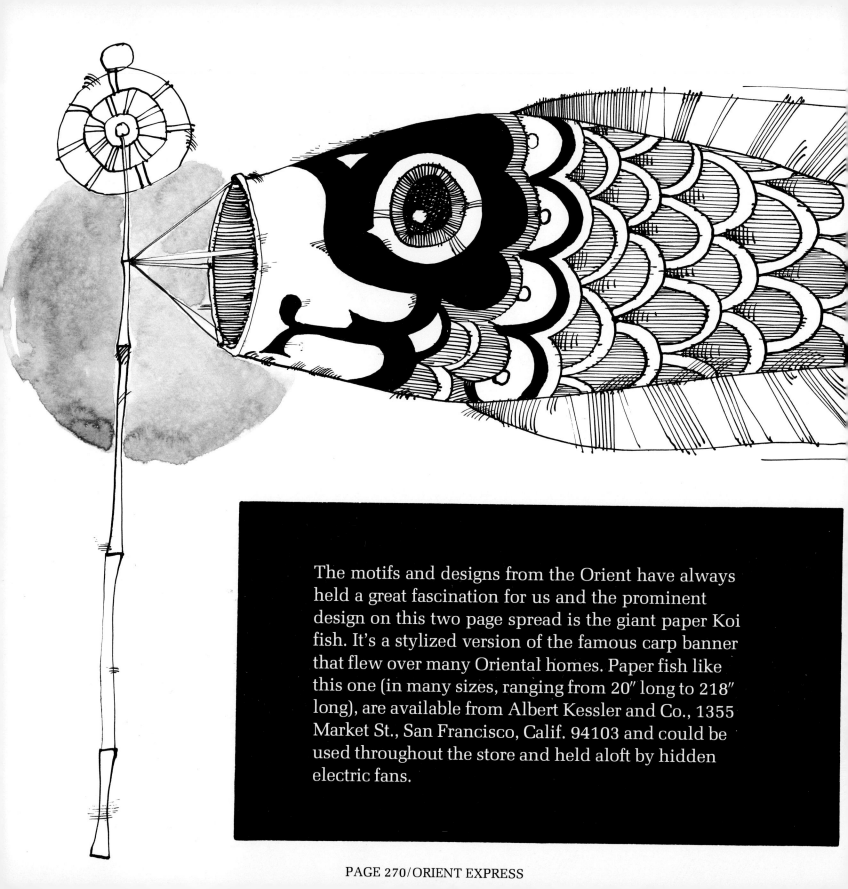

The motifs and designs from the Orient have always held a great fascination for us and the prominent design on this two page spread is the giant paper Koi fish. It's a stylized version of the famous carp banner that flew over many Oriental homes. Paper fish like this one (in many sizes, ranging from 20″ long to 218″ long), are available from Albert Kessler and Co., 1355 Market St., San Francisco, Calif. 94103 and could be used throughout the store and held aloft by hidden electric fans.

We are offering two different window display ideas. The banner version on the left incorporates a raw wooden frame filled with polished river stones with the "T" bar supported by a bamboo pole. From the bar are four graphic banners made from Upson Duo White 2 or felt. The panelized display shown on this page can be treated in many different ways. Some panels can be made using pine framing, stained to resemble teak or painted in bright colors of lacquer. Some frames can carry thick transluscent parchment or rice papers with Chinese calligraphy and design symbols drawn on. The design for the charming "Yahata" horse was inspired by the same kind of Japanese folk toys shown in the picture on page 277. This giant horse can be made from Upson and decorated in traditional design patterns.

Using Upson Duo White 2 again, with brass or plastic rings, we have formed this unusual hanging divider for use in a shop or as a background device for windows.

On a walk in New York City, we happened upon the China Book and Periodical Shop at 125 Fifth Avenue. One of the fascinating items they were selling were hand cut paper prints. Some in multi-colors and others in plain bright colors. The photostats shown are same size and each open area has been skillfully cut by hand. We have found them fascinating as an amazing folk craft and as reference for design.

Mr. Lester J. Brooks, Director of Art Originals Ltd., 43 Marshall Ridge Rd., New Canaan, Conn. 06840, has been most cooperative in supplying us with these examples of Japanese folk toys. They range from the famous hand crafted sano-bari (literally: wooden birds), made by peasant families in rural Japan. A centuries old traditional folk art, each bird is carved from a single piece of wood, ruffled feathers and all. Each bird is a family affair. Grandfather chops the tree, Father's steady hand carve the birds, Mother paints them, and the children pack each one individually in beautiful simulated cedar boxes.

In addition to these unusual wood carvings are beautiful papier-mache dolls and other unusual wooden and clay items.

PANELS

When you think of panels — think of Upson, as we offer so much to the panel maker — flexibility — lightweight strength — different thicknesses — sizes — paintability, plus the surface to take wallpaper and other decorative treatment.

Upson panels are easy to work with and lend themselves to all types of fastening devices — glue — nails — staples and Upson invisible fasteners. Many projects call for quick rugged panels and we've discovered a simple and inexpensive way to make up panels of different thicknesses and heights depending upon the width of the special dadoed frame that you make for them. The illustrations on the right illustrates how the dado works — a recessed groove to carry the Upson panel.

The photos also show four ways to make your Upson panels thick and rugged, yet featherweight by the square foot.

- A. Kraft honeycomb — ideal for its lightweight feature combined with extraordinary strength laterally.
- B. Styrafoam "batts" glued at 12' or 16' intervals will support the panel inside.
- C. Egg crating made of Upson serves as support for panels of various thicknesses. Merely cut the Upson in bands the same height as the dimension left by the two recessing dados.
- D. Small wooden blocks can be cut to the same height and glued in place.

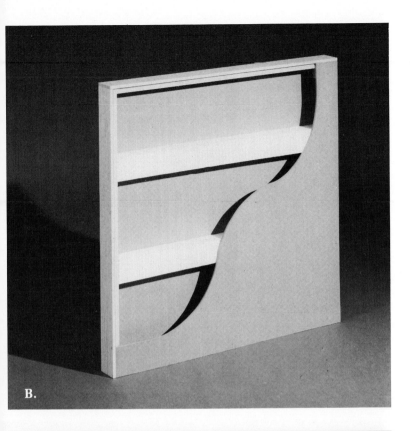

B.

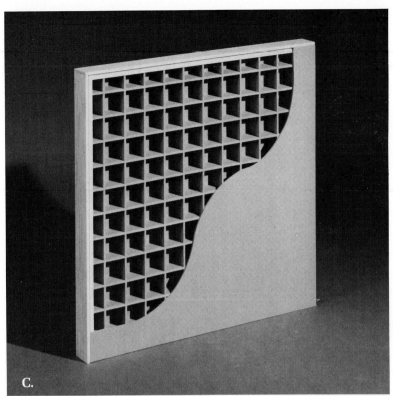

C.

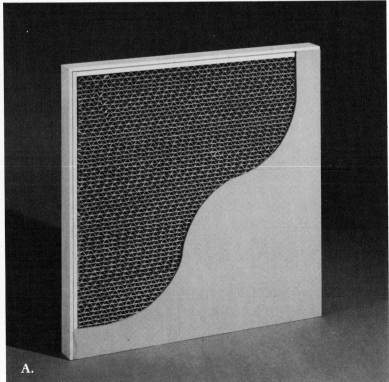

A.

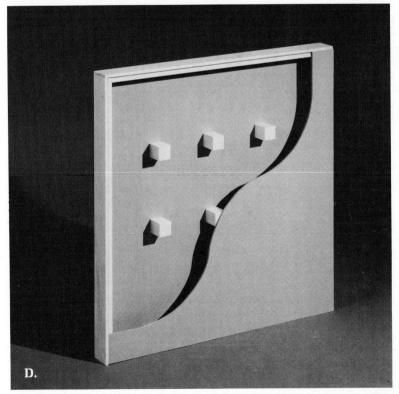

D.

flex-y-panels

Every displayer and exhibit builder is interested in a low cost, fully constructed, unpainted panel and we think we have found an excellent source for you. Flex-Y-Plan Industries have worked out a low cost rigid 4 x 8 panel that sells for about $21.50 each. They are 1¾″ thick with a kraft honeycomb core, particle board framing and surfaced on both sides with Upson Easy-Curve. Each panel weighs approximately 36 pounds and can be finished in any kind of media. Panels can be joined with simple bed hardware, steel flanges, etc. Also available in 2′ x 8′ panels. Minimum orders 1 package in any one of the following standard packages: 6-4 x 8, 5-4 x 8, 4-4 x 8, 3-4 x 8, 2-2 x 8, 4-2 x 8, 6-2 x 8, 2-4 x 8, 1-4 x 8, 12-2 x 8, 8-2 x 8, 10-2 x 8. Source: Flex-Y-Plan Industries, 2669 W. 17th Street, P.O. Box 8341, Erie, Penna. 16505.

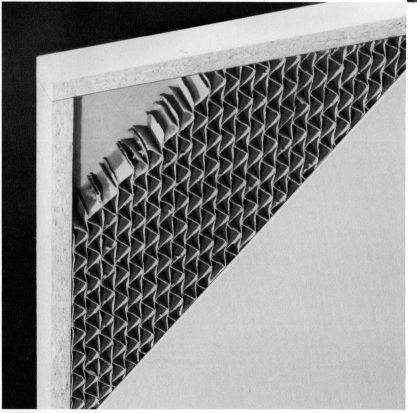

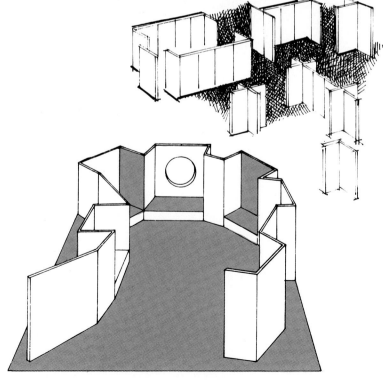

Papers

Large rolls of beautifully designed wrapping paper are available all over the country, but we would like to recommend an amazing group of beautifully designed papers from Faroy Sales, P.O. Box 36446, Houston, Texas 77036.

On the pages 282, 283, and 284 we have illustrated 12 typical designs and it's a pity that we could not illustrate them in full color. On page 285 and 286 we have shown 14 different ways that they can be used. Although the examples pertain mainly to home decorating, we feel there are countless ways that beautiful papers like these can be used in display. Covering huge cubes or tubes, stapling them to backgrounds and even cutting shapes out of them and gluing them to the surface of your display. The designs shown are 3' x 4', 24 rolls per design per carton.

Rubaiyat — full color

Malachite — Shades of green and black

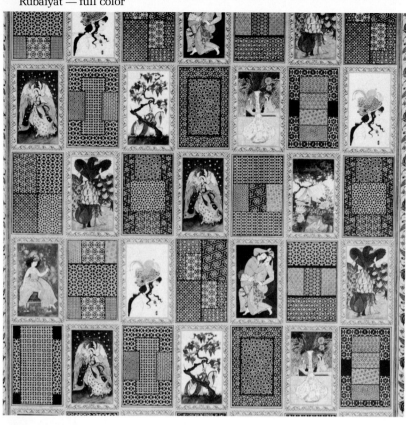

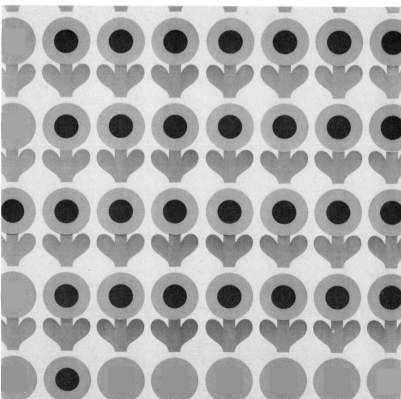

Modern pattern 153 — full color

Toile — Dark Red or blue on cream

Jungle — full color

Dolls — Full color

Facade — Full color

Art Glass — Full Color

Bacchinal — black on rust, tan on silver blue

Nouveau — Reds, blues, greens, golds, black and whi

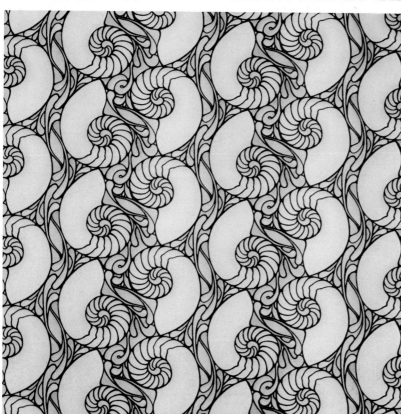

Nautilus — muted colors and black

Friends — black and white on blue or green

As described in our introduction, the 14 photographs that appear on the next two pages are excellent examples of how these Faroy papers can be used in home decoration and as we explained, the display possibilities are endless.

Penny Candy

With the renewed interest in nostalgia, what could be more packed with memories than the old drug stores and the places where we used to buy penny candy? On another New York stroll, we found an enchanting Penny Candy Store on Madison Avenue and it was a small shop with literally dozens of tin lidded jars, each containing a different kind of candy.

The introductory page illustrates our idea of a Penny Candy Shop, using the shape of an old fashioned gum ball machine. Certainly, the forms shown on these two pages could be used for many other promotions — children shops, as shapes over a regular candy counter, etc. The beautiful jumbo jars are from Wheaton Products, Millville, N.J. 08332. They are available in round top and diamond top styles ranging in size from 4½″ to 13½″. Write for their current styles and prices.

At the right is an array of jars, candies and scoops from Penny Lane Sweet Shoppe, 39 Stringham Ave., Valley Stream, N.Y. 11580. They specialize in selling penny candy in bulk and have many unusual merchandising plans available. Ye Olde Sweet Cart is an aisle merchandiser, their Mini-Sweet Shop is a wall type merchandiser and they also specialize in installations of Penny Candy stores in the University market.

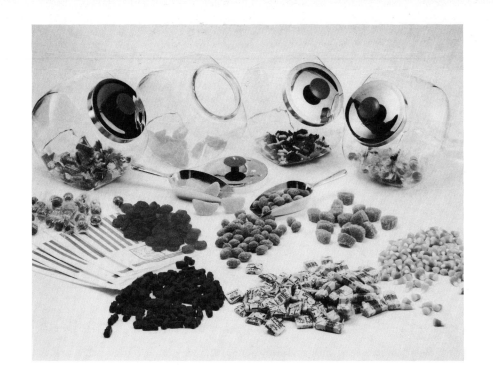

We thought the four photographs on page 291 would be of interest to you. The old fashioned candy store glass storage jars are from Faroy Sales, P.O. Box 36446, Houston, Texas 77036. The candles on trays in the form of strawberry tarts and pastries are also from Faroy and could be an excellent "line of merchandise" to carry in your "Candy Store". In the upper right hand corner is a clever sign made from Upson Easy Curve incorporating Mitten's Showboat letters with 8 different kinds of penny candy held by plexi-glas. The photo in the lower right hand corner is from the Upson photo library and dates back to 1919, illustrating how effectively Upson ceiling panels looked in this old fashioned candy store.

THE POTTING SHED

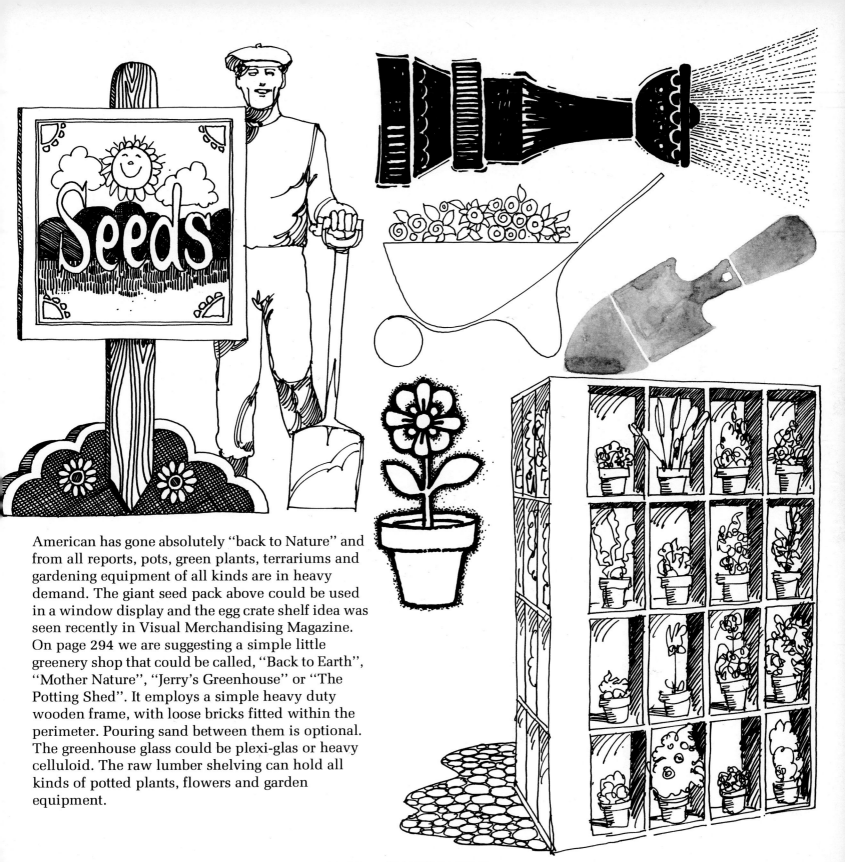

American has gone absolutely "back to Nature" and from all reports, pots, green plants, terrariums and gardening equipment of all kinds are in heavy demand. The giant seed pack above could be used in a window display and the egg crate shelf idea was seen recently in Visual Merchandising Magazine. On page 294 we are suggesting a simple little greenery shop that could be called, "Back to Earth", "Mother Nature", "Jerry's Greenhouse" or "The Potting Shed". It employs a simple heavy duty wooden frame, with loose bricks fitted within the perimeter. Pouring sand between them is optional. The greenhouse glass could be plexi-glas or heavy celluloid. The raw lumber shelving can hold all kinds of potted plants, flowers and garden equipment.

flowers

PLEXI-GLAS

SHELVING FOR
FLORAL DISPLAYS

WOODEN FLOOR

HEAVY WOODEN FRAME

THIS WAY
TO THE
GREEN THUMB
NURSERY

Taylor & NG, 489th Street, San Francisco, Calif. 94103, specializes in unusual items for gardeners, besides carrying an extensive line of cookware, woks, and other Chinese cooking utensils. Their catalog is fascinating.

Potpourri

When the Upson Company produced the first four idea books we spent a great deal of time on unusual promotions and realizing that these books and poster sets are out of print, we thought it would be helpful to reproduce 28 of the best pages for your enjoyment.

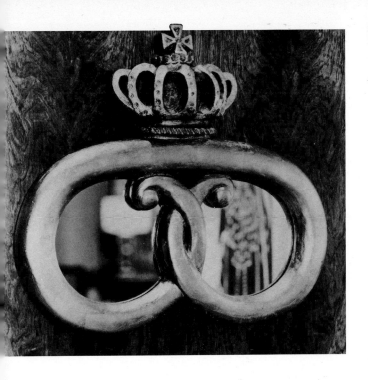

SKÄLs SHOP

GLÄS

DANI

DENMARK

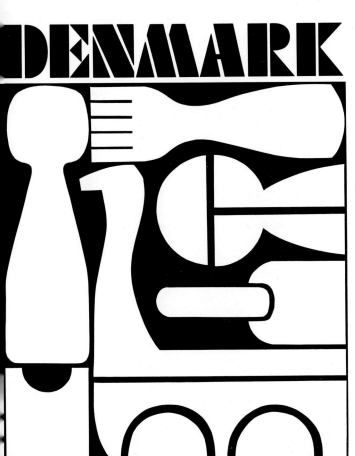

NORSK

Four pages from an older Danish promotion. Many of these ideas can be used in connection with the Vikingsholm Section, starting on page 395. The Royal Baker Shop sign is from the Jo Mead collection, 17 North Elizabeth, Chicago, Ill. 60607.

These four pages from the Italian promotion illustrate the variety of design. Gallery West is a panelized display that could feature Italian crafts.

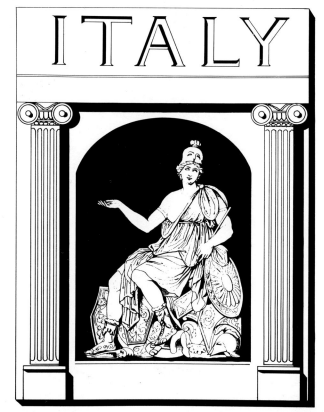

FRANCE

Wine is the feature in this promotion. The bottle shape was achieved with corks from the local Hardware Store and Mitten's letters. The wines of France display idea could be achieved by forming huge corks of Upson Easy Curve, painting them to simulate cork or covering them with actual cork sheets or cork surface contact paper.

Vintage '76

Our London promotion from one of our older books can tie in with the Londonderry promotion, starting on page 257. The key display here is the Dover Sole display, using 4 wooden crates and "stencil-like" printing to lend an import feeling to the promotion. The Crown is from Jo Mead Designs.

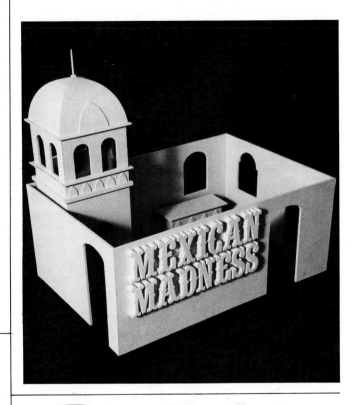

Mexican Madness is our idea for a shop within a shop. It uses a tower and court yard idea to form a Mexican Boutique. The motifs of Mexico have afforded us much in terms of intricate designs and unusual constructions. We have shown several wall plaques that can be formed from Upson and the huge tin lantern can be used as a central piece for your Mexican displays.

Each display of these displays has a California style. We especially like the gigantic Tiffany lamps that could be produced from Easy Curve, using die-cut holes, backed with colored tissue or plastic. Imagine three of these giants hanging from the ceiling of the first floor in your store, setting the stage for your Tiffany era promotion.

HOLIDAYS

AMERICANA

With so much emphasis on Nationalism all over the world, what better place to start than in America. Eagles, Indians, apple pie, baseball, old locomotives, Holidays, seasons and Back to School, all in one super design. Additional Americana is shown in the Almanac Section, starting on page 23 and more holidays are shown on page 229.

Photopotpourri

We have all heard the expression "There is nothing new under the sun" and we also refer to another beautiful phrase that is found on page 253 — "To see what everyone has seen and think what no one has thought".

We firmly believe that to be truly productive in any career requires that we surround ourselves with literally tons of reference. We maintain elaborate reference files, plus, scores of good reference books and last, but not least, we like to keep an up to date photo file. On every trip a trusty Instamatic (the new pocket ones are terrific) and a compact Minox are always packed.

On the next 15 pages we have shown 90 random pictures from the files. Some might seem farfetched, but in our view all are fascinating and useful.

Ceramic china displayed with their original crates and excelsior.

A nice small window using boxes.

The Occult exhibit at the Hallmark Gallery

Giant forms for impact

The fun and games exhibit — Hallmark

A tube and a rectangular shape form a Santa.

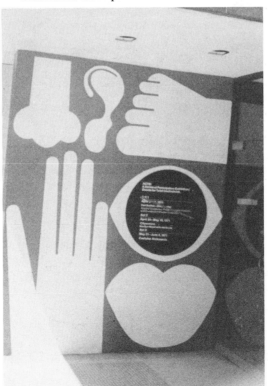

P. J. Clarks — New York

Yorkville, Toronto

A dimensional awning sign

Expo— Montreal

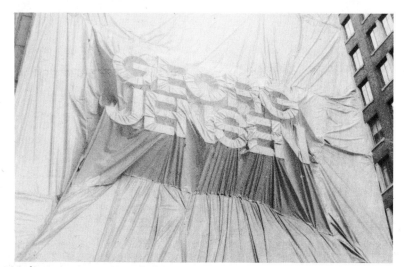

Madison Avenue — New York City

Hamilton, Ontario

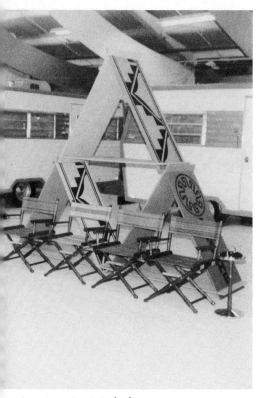

An interesting interlock

Fiber glass Exhibit — New York

Giant prints at Time/Life

Georg Jensen — New York

Boxes and boxes

More Fiber glass modules

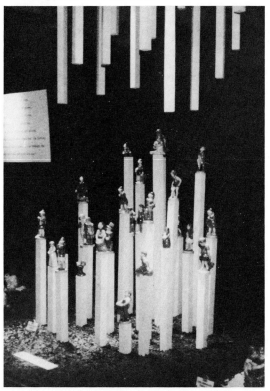

A novel wine rack

The penny farthing

The toy collector

More of Jerry Smith's toys

An Armstrong exhibit

Sleds and sleighs

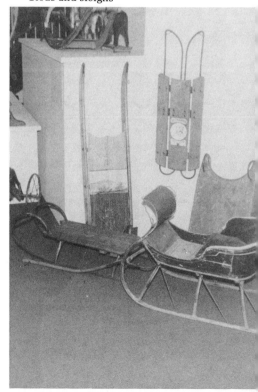

Paper tubes and connectors

A clever promotional idea

A great way to use plastic coffee measures

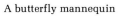

A butterfly mannequin

Adams & Yves

An ornate chair — Detroit Institute of Art

Sculpture Show — Toronto

More of the same

Segal-like figures over a doorway

Toronto International Airport

A butterfly sculpture

Chapin Hall Park School

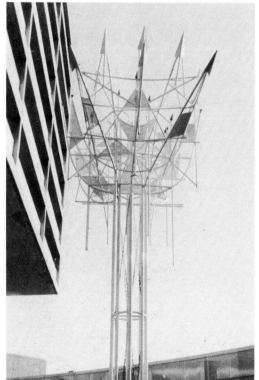

A circular window

New York City Restaurant Sign

615 Second Avenue, New York

A good restaurant — Toronto

Sleepin' at the grab bag

Smart graphics

New York brownstone

Gingerbread widow's walk

An abandoned schoolhouse — Western New York

Louis Sullivan detail of the facade of the Carson Pirie Scott & Co. Dept. Store — Chicago.

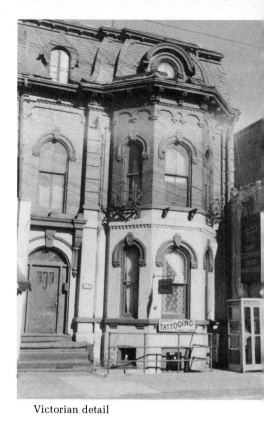

Victorian detail

A touch of the Ukraine — St. Catharines, Ontario

A good use of different sized windows

Eaton's Anniversary window/Toronto

An exterior treatment — Eaton's

A richly detailed wall — Minneapolis

Detroit Institute of Art

A good name for an antique shop

Penny Candy Anyone?

Boxes on a wa

Super graphics — Toronto

Erie County Fair in Hamburg, New Yor

Stylized forms of London

Great reference for a fire sal

nice touch for your Adobe promotion

A Kidsworld idea

nterlock Panels

A polaroid exhibit made entirely of printed
white corrugated

lice stylized graphics

Unusual dimensional letters

American Almanac

Flower wreaths — Descending size

Simpson Sears at Christmas time

A shot from across the stre

Stoneware wall decor on natural wood

This Giraffe lost his carous

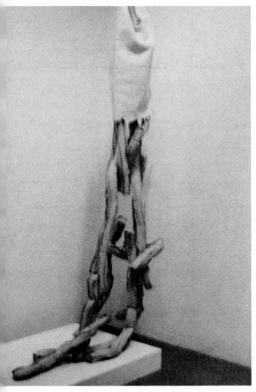
Claes Oldenberg's "Shoestring Potatoes"

Frank Stella at his best

More Toronto sculpture

Simple but nice

A richly detailed door in New York

Davenport Road, Canada

FINE FRENCH FURNITURE

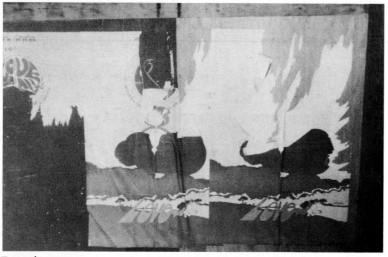

Torn play posters

Henry Moore's "Archer"

A Nun on skates

The mighty Niagara

Marshall Field's famous clock

A church on the way to Paris, Ontario

clever doll display

A shop — Cambridge, Mass.

closeup of a wall at CBS, N.Y.C.

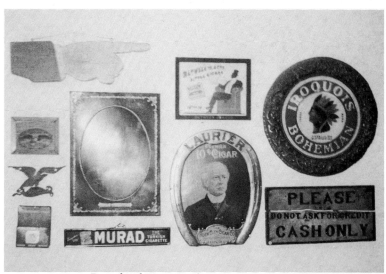

Part of Wil Hayett's advertising antiques collection in N.Y.C.

e like cabooses

A clever exhibit in fresh bright colors

RUSSIAN EASTER

If the Yves St. Laurant spring collection is any indication The Russians really are coming with buttoned-on-the-shoulder cossack shirts, long quilted coats, easter egg bright colors, Russian aviator hats and high boots.

With the new interest in Russian styles and the easing of trade, retail stores have taken a new look at this important influence. Many structural forms can be used for your promotion, ranging from the onion shaped domes of medieval and Byzantine churches to ornate stoves, troikas and the famous Ukrainian Easter eggs painted by the peasants.

Pysanky

When you make your own Pysanky you will want them to be both beautiful and authentic. They will be if, besides following the instructions carefully, you become familiar with the traditions and beliefs associated with Pysanky.

The decoration of Easter eggs has been a Ukrainian tradition for over ten centuries. At one time, the egg was associated with pagan rituals and superstitions. In 988, the Ukraine accepted Christianity, the decoration of eggs took on a deep religious meaning. The decorated eggs commemorated the Resurrection of Christ and the pagan superstitions were replaced by religious beliefs and legends.

One of the legends most familiar in Ukraine tells of a poor peddler who was on his way to market to sell a basket of eggs when he met an angry crowd. The crowd was mocking a man staggering beneath the weight of a cross, and the poor peddler, taking pity on him, left his basket by the roadside and went to the man's assistance. The man was Christ, the peddler was Simon, and the eggs were the first Pysanky.

Although no two Pysanky are exactly alike, there are certain basic designs and methods of arranging them. Individuality is achieved by varying combinations of design and color.

The egg is always divided into basic fields by lines running horizontally and/or vertically around the egg. The same design is placed in each field. Secondary divisions divide the original fields into smaller sections in which individual parts of the design are placed.

The motifs are divided into three categories, Geometric, animal and plant. Below we have shown a wide cross section of these designs.

The eggs shown in the photograph are from the collection of J. Marian Boraczok, Buffalo, New York.

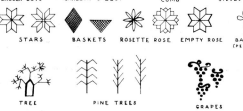

LADDER DOTS   & RIBBON & BELT   RAKE COMB   SIEVES

STARS   BASKETS   ROSETTE ROSE   EMPTY ROSE   BARVINOK (PERIWINKLE)

TREE   PINE TREES   GRAPES

CROSSES   SPOONS SPIDERWEB POPPY EYES

HORNS   MAIDENS COAL AX SPIDER BUTTERFLY FISH   RAM'S HORNS HEN'S FEET

REINDEER   SPARROW   GOOSE FEET

HORSE   ROOSTER   HEN

shellgame

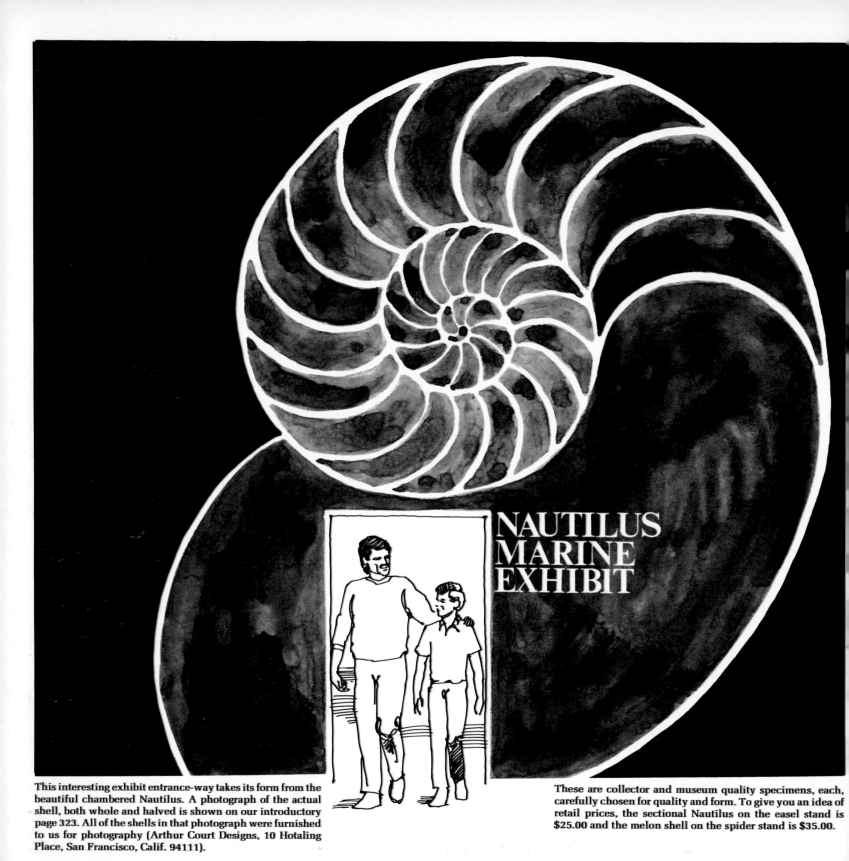

NAUTILUS
MARINE
EXHIBIT

This interesting exhibit entrance-way takes its form from the beautiful chambered Nautilus. A photograph of the actual shell, both whole and halved is shown on our introductory page 323. All of the shells in that photograph were furnished to us for photography (Arthur Court Designs, 10 Hotaling Place, San Francisco, Calif. 94111).

These are collector and museum quality specimens, each, carefully chosen for quality and form. To give you an idea of retail prices, the sectional Nautilus on the easel stand is $25.00 and the melon shell on the spider stand is $35.00.

Giant shell shapes can be cut from Upson and mounted on back walls or made into 36″ square plaques to hang from the ceiling.

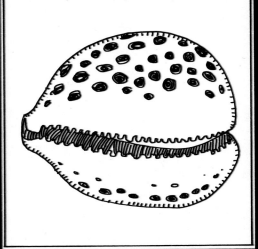

Shops
and boutiques

On the next 13 pages we have presented a random group of ideas for individual shops, shops within the store and boutiques. Many are self explanatary and each of them can start you thinking about other promotions, etc. Size and scale are important and as far as materials are concerned "the sky is the limit".

The sun shop form
really belongs back in
the Summer Stock section, but
it blended so nicely on this page that we
placed it here. This could double as a merchandiser
and a sign with hangers hung from a rod under the
flat area on the left hand side. The Market on the Mall could
be lettering painted directly on a bushel basket top or the top
could be simulated in giant form and hung from the ceiling, or in a
half circle archway.

The Wind Up Mouse is one of our favorites and could be used in a dozen different ways, as a Children's shop, a small section selling mechanical toys only or as a complete toy shop. Paperteria is self explanatory, Mitten's Standees mounted in front of the different colored Upson clouds.

The Wind-up Mouse.

RAZZA·MA·TAZZ

DIFFERENT COLORED PAPERS MOUNTED ON UPSON BOARD EACH BOARD STANDS INDEPENDANTLY AND LIT FROM BELOW

MITTENS

PAPERTERIA

A quintet of signs. A large form can be cut for the
wool sign and actual large colored yarn could be
wrapped around the form with a large paper band to
simulate the skein label.

WOOL

THE WORLD'S WURST SHOP

ETCETERA ETCETERA

pinwheel

buttons

fall fashion firsts

It is very obvious that we like Mitten's Letters. We have found them most compatable with Upson and the few pages that follow will give you an idea of their versatility. Intermingled with the sign ideas are several shop construction designs that might be of help to you. The spectacular wall shown above was produced for the Madison Square Garden branch of the Chemical Bank in New York and while other people are visiting the Empire State Building you ought to drop in and see this beauty during banking hours. It combines dimensional symbols of objects and names associated with Madison Square Garden and New York land-marks. Every size and style of Mitten's Letters have been used. (Mitten's Designer Letters, 85 Fifth Ave., New York 10003).

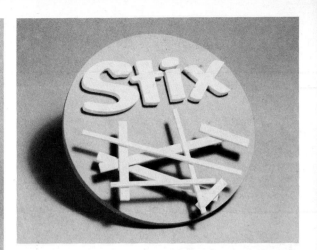

Felt, an artist's mannequin, plaster, baskets and wood. All have been used in this interesting group of signs.

Eight more signs using different materials. Actual brass items are attached to the background on the Brix and Brass sign and four different kinds of Pasta were used in little compartments for the Pasta plaque.

A refinished old cabinet door makes a beautiful background.

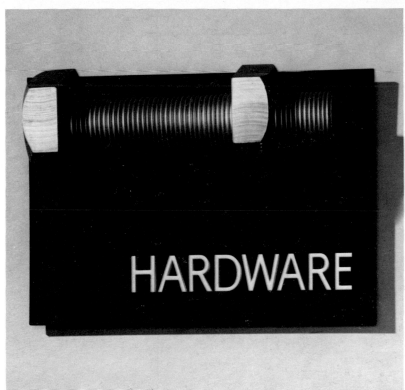

A gigantic hand turned wooden bolt, finished in glossy aluminum paint.

Actual barn board provides a rustic feeling.

A lobster painted in acrylics on a beach-worn chair seat.

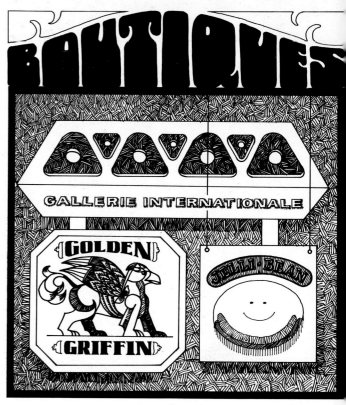

Twenty five little ideas from a recent Upson book.

Summer Stuff

SUN SEASON

A dimensional sun form would be effective as a window display piece or near the entrance of a small merchandise shop.

TOP OF THE POPS SUMMER FASHION SHOW.

ICE CREAM COLORS

An ice cream colors promotion could be centered around the form of an old crank style ice cream freezer with giant waves of color coming from the top. These could be made from large pieces of Upson Easy Curve and painted with latex paints or with actual fabric.

We have predicted, along with many other retailers, that this is the year of the watermelon. The motif pops up repeatedly in chairs, children's clothes, place mats, pillows, etc. On the next three pages we are showing you the results of a design group brain-storming session to see how many different displays, merchandisers and tables we could form using the watermelon motif.

COOL COOL SUMMER FASHIONS

Hot pinks, fuschias, lipstick reds and black are the predominant colors produced in many different finishes including vinyl, felt, colored papers and paint. Large hemispheres, in Machine Mache are available from Century Displays, 1200 S. Figueroa St., Los Angeles, Calif. 90015. The promotion can be used for women's, children's and teenage clothing, cosmetics, gifts and housewares.

Suppliers

The word supplier is really a misnomer. As we stated in o[ur] introduction to the Supplier Section in Upson's Book of t[he] World, "As work progressed and design sketches were comi[ng] into final form we realized that the real value of any display [is] the final surface treatment and the atmosphere created".

We are very proud of our quality line of Upson fibreboards f[or] display and we are also proud that we offer the greatest varie[ty] to choose from.

This particular Supplier Source section has been formed, n[ot] because we couldn't find a specific promotional section [to] assign them, but that many items here apply to many sections [of] the book.

We also have offered within this section of the book, beautif[ul] paper tissue items from Amscan, just because we really li[ke] them and we feel they have a type of intrinsic charm that is n[ot] easily found. *Let There Be Neon* is an unusual supplier sour[ce] and it really is offered to prompt some great ideas as far as yo[ur] display and promotions are concerned.

All Culver Prints are in the category of "A Rare Breed". They a[re] one of a very few archive libraries existing in the U.S. today an[d] so, when you think of promotion they become, along with Ne[on] Lights and Creegan animated figures, important and possib[le] segments of your total promotion.

Upson has not charged firms mentioned in this book. In almo[st] all cases we made the initial contact after seeing their produc[ts] in consumer and trade magazines, direct mail pieces an[d] learning about them by word of mouth. Naturally, we welcom[e] any interest from any manufacturer, craftsman, supplier, etc. [at] any time for possible exposure in future Upson books an[d] publications. We will enjoy hearing from you at any time.

A good example of an excellent supplier in our view is T[he] Yankee Collection, mentioned on Page 44. We saw a tiny ad [in] House and Garden magazine, sent our quarter and receive[d] their very charming catalog. Just this simple action had de[-]veloped into a full page exposure for that firm.

We feel this is a valuable service and when everyone connect[ed] directly or indirectly with the display field realizes that we ca[n] all work together, then the industry itself prospers.

PEBBLED UPSONITE

Pebbled Upsonite boards come in three useful thicknesses: 3/8″ for those big display jobs that take strength and rigidity and 3/16″ for small jobs. The subtle pebbled top surface cuts easily, sands beautifully and takes paint like a pro.

3/16″ is available —
    4′ x 6′, 8′, 10′, 12′
1/4″ is available —
    4′ x 8′, 10′, 12′
3/8″ is available — 4′ x 8′
Address for all six Upson products is on the back cover.

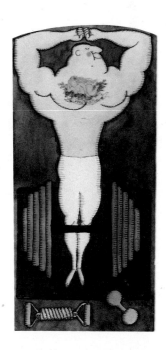

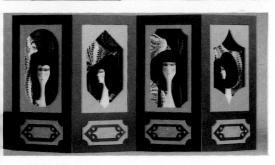

UPSONITE
EASY CURVE

Easy Curve is the graceful panel board. It is loaded with flexibility and adaptability. It is made of long fibre material that can bend or roll into columns as small as 10″ in diameter. It molds to framing to form display articles of your own imaginative creations. It has a three ply, laminated construction that measures approximately ⅛″ thick. Strong, but so easy to cut with a knife or Cutawl. Paints beautifully with all kinds of media. Available in 4′ wide by 8′ long panels.

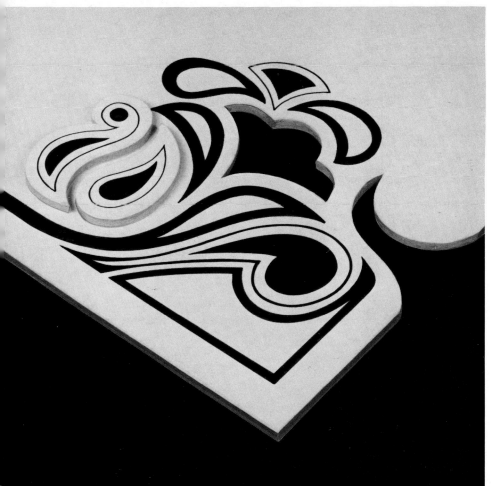

UPSONITE
DUO WHITE

Here is a brilliant display board with a nice white surface on both sides. Easy to cut, supreme in paintability. This super smoothie is the bright way to display.

It's often called the Royal Display Board. A perfect surface for silk screening without crawling or soaking in. Excellent for fine filigree work, cut-outs and appliques.

Duo White 2 is a five ply laminated board, ³⁄₁₆″ thick, available in 4 x 8 panels.

UPSON
$\frac{3}{16}$" UNIVERSAL

Universal is the practical choice of designers where both economy and versatility are needed. We call it the board of 1001 uses. Uniform in structure and quality, Universal cuts easily with a knife, saw or cutawl and is ideal for models, small displays, big backgrounds and picture mounting.

Universal die cuts to close tolerances without ragged or broken edges. It is available in 4' x 8' panels, ³⁄₁₆" thick, smooth two sides.

LINEN FINISH UPSONITE

This classic panel is embossed with linen texture on one side and smooth on the other. Its cut and color qualities give that professional touch to any display or art rendering. The "canvas-look" surface has excellent tooth and satisfies the most exacting artist. Available in 4' x 8' panels — ³⁄₁₆" thick.

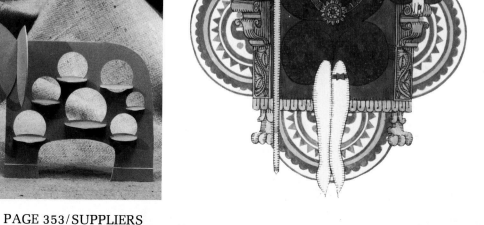

UPSON
ALL WEATHER
PANELS FOR DISPLAYS AND EXHIBITS

Bigness is a powerful attraction in display. It is also one of the unique features of Upson All Weather Panels. Available in standard 4′ widths and also in giant 8′ wide panels in 12′ and 16′ lengths. It must be understood that these large panels are seldom stocked locally and the best approach is to contact local lumber dealers handling Upson.

Upson All Weather Panels are formed by laminating six woodfibre plys into a 3⁄8″ thick board, rugged and strong, for use in all kinds of weight-bearing displays, both interior and exterior. When two panels are glued together they form an excellent material for thick cut-out letters and all kinds of detailed scroll work, as shown in the photograph in the lower right. All Weather comes unprimed one side for exterior signs and displays.

The wrecking Bar, 2601 McKinney Avenue, Dallas, Texas 75204, was named after the famous tool needed to remove the beautiful architechtural antiques that they offer. The business was founded by Mr. and Mrs. Kenneth McDonald, to satisfy their love for old architectural remnants and to supply commodities of this type, not readily available when wanted. Their offerings cover a wide range of styles including old mantels, lighting fixtures ranging from Georgian brass to elaborately carved chandeliers, plus French, American and English stained glass, old Southern cypress shutters, porcelain bar room fixtures and other ornamental elements.

The basement is a treasure trove of iron gates, English and French shop fronts and transplanted building facades.

Provost Displays, Inc., 618 West 28th Street, New York 10001. This interesting firm offers an unusual service with its Kustom-Wall. This is a vacuum formed wall panel in giant size (up to 4′ x 12′) that can reproduce your trademarks, special lettering and any other dimensional object that can be placed into the design. When completed the material is a rigid, high impact vinyl plastic and can be nailed, stapled or glued on back panels, etc.

This firm also carries a wide variety of standard plastic panels, including Pecky cypress, Spanish rough tile, Cedar shingle, English brick and clapboard. Brochures and prices are available by writing to Charles (Chick) Provost.

The art of producing honeycomb tissue fold-out display pieces has been with us for years and we are especially impressed with the Amscan line. The variety is unlimited and we have found the design and construction of the highest quality. Write for their newest catalog, covering hundreds of subjects.

Amscan Incorporated, South Road, Harrison, N.Y. 10528.

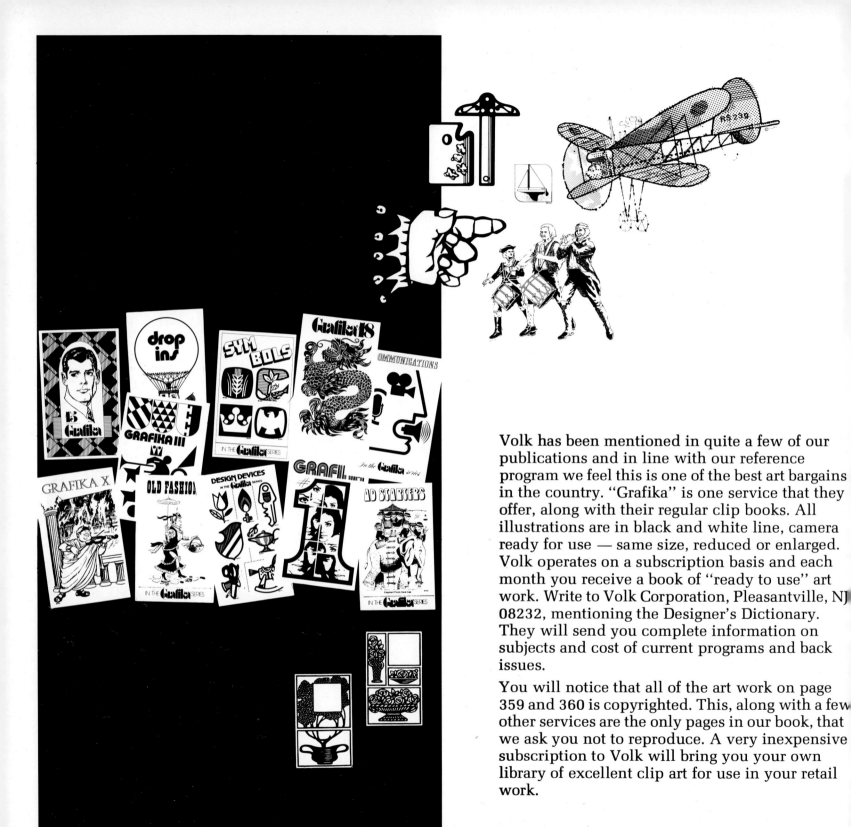

Volk has been mentioned in quite a few of our publications and in line with our reference program we feel this is one of the best art bargains in the country. "Grafika" is one service that they offer, along with their regular clip books. All illustrations are in black and white line, camera ready for use — same size, reduced or enlarged. Volk operates on a subscription basis and each month you receive a book of "ready to use" art work. Write to Volk Corporation, Pleasantville, NJ 08232, mentioning the Designer's Dictionary. They will send you complete information on subjects and cost of current programs and back issues.

You will notice that all of the art work on page 359 and 360 is copyrighted. This, along with a few other services are the only pages in our book, that we ask you not to reproduce. A very inexpensive subscription to Volk will bring you your own library of excellent clip art for use in your retail work.

Looking for instant money?

HIT THE JACK POT

Produce a little more; produce it a little better!

HEAR YE! HEAR YE!

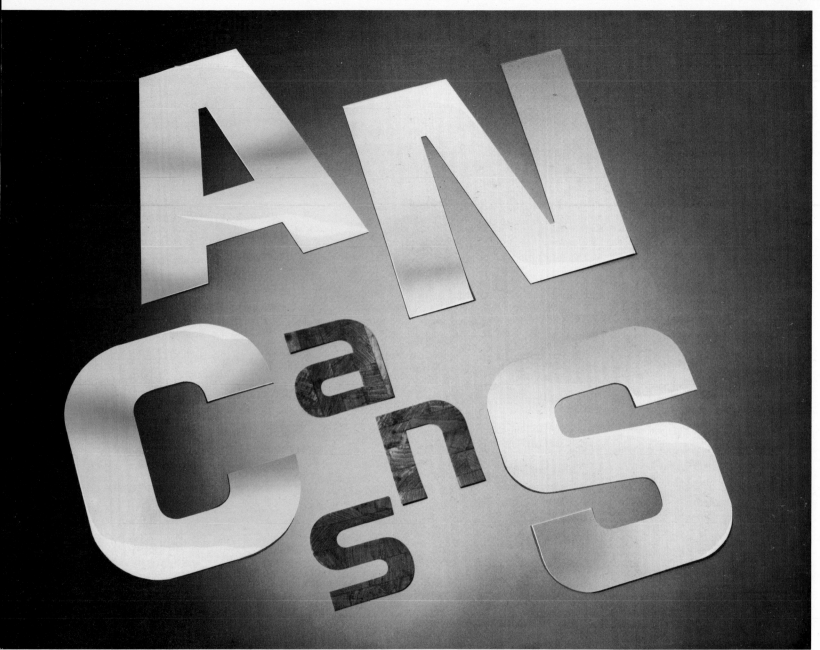

Astro Studio, 4270 West First Street, Los Angeles, Calif. 90004, offers an unusual line of die-cut letters in various styles of pressure sensitive stock that can be adhered to many types of surfaces. They offer white matte finish, black patent, silver, gold, cork, and a variety of solid colors. We thought their butcher block pattern would be a rich addition to the Carvery Display in the Gourmet Section, black vinyl letters spelling Fromage in the Cheese Section and the rich cork pattern is extremely appropriate for the American Adobe signs. Write for price and samples.

Quality animation is a rare thing to find and we think the design group at Creegan Products Co., 508 Seventh St., Stuebenville, Ohio 43952, lead the field.

Quoting from their brochure, "The Creegan Company specializes in retail traffic building, using puppet theatre animations and the newest in display techniques". Some of their shopping center attractions are Pinocchio, Raggedy Ann, Yum Yum Village and African Safari and two special productions that are extremely timely, "A Yankee Doodle Holiday" and "A Colonial America 1776". Their other offerings are animation figures in individual units and theme groups, including Warner Brother cartoon characters and puppet productions (Sleeping Bunny, The Littlest Snow Man, The Talking Christmas Tree, etc.).

Address inquiries to George R. Creegan mentioning The Designer's Dictionary.

451 West Broadway · New York City · 10012
Phone: (212) 473-8630

RUDI STERN · CHARLES SCHWARTZ

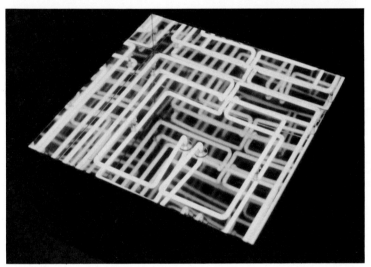

To Rudi Stern, a Manhattan lighting designer, "Neon signs are more than glaring advertisements. They are an anonymous art form, that is indelibly part of the American landscape, as important a part of us as our highway system" But Neon signs are rapidly being replaced by more modern forms of outdoor advertising, and to prevent the complete disappearance of Neon from the American scene Stern has decided to move indoors. He has opened a Manhattan gallery called, "Let There Be Neon". The interesting aspect of this gallery, as far as we are concerned, is the unusual service that they are offering with unique portable and interchangeable Neon signs. They are able to produce names in Neon, Logos, Symbols and special point of purchase displays.

Contact them for current prices on Neon premiums.

As designers, we have always been very enthusiastic about archive prints and photographs. Culver Pictures, 660 First Avenue, New York 10016, has a magnificent collection and by their own testimony claim to be the countries oldest and largest historic picture archive: (6½ million photographs, prints and engravings).

We have used six beautiful examples in the Almanac Section starting on page 34 and others are sprinkled throughout the book. We are indebted to Roberts Jackson for his cooperation in allowing us to reproduce these examples. Their major categories are business, family, history, movie stills, performing arts, personality, recreation and sports, science and invention, transportation and miscellaneous.

This unique firm places a major resource at your service. Write for their illustrated Picture Guide, (shown above) available for $2.50.

P.S. Please remember that the prints shown in our book have been loaned to us and cannot be reproduced, without a fee paid to Culver.

Susan Crane, 8107 Chancellor Row, Dallas, Texas 75247, is a firm specializing in visual merchandising ideas for stores and they also specialize in custom designed corporate identity programs, and custom gift packaging. On these two pages we have shown natural Americana, an example of a total store promotion. As the numbers indicate the program covers all aspects of retail merchandising from shopping totes and gift wraps to coordinated merchandisers, display cubes and back panels. Write for complete details.

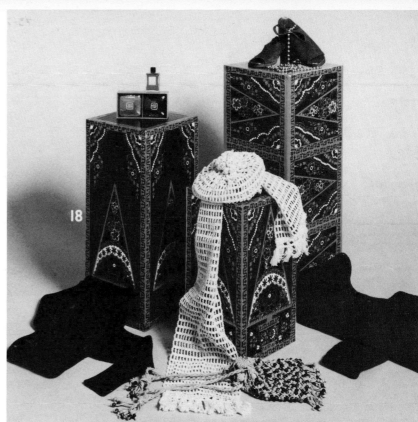

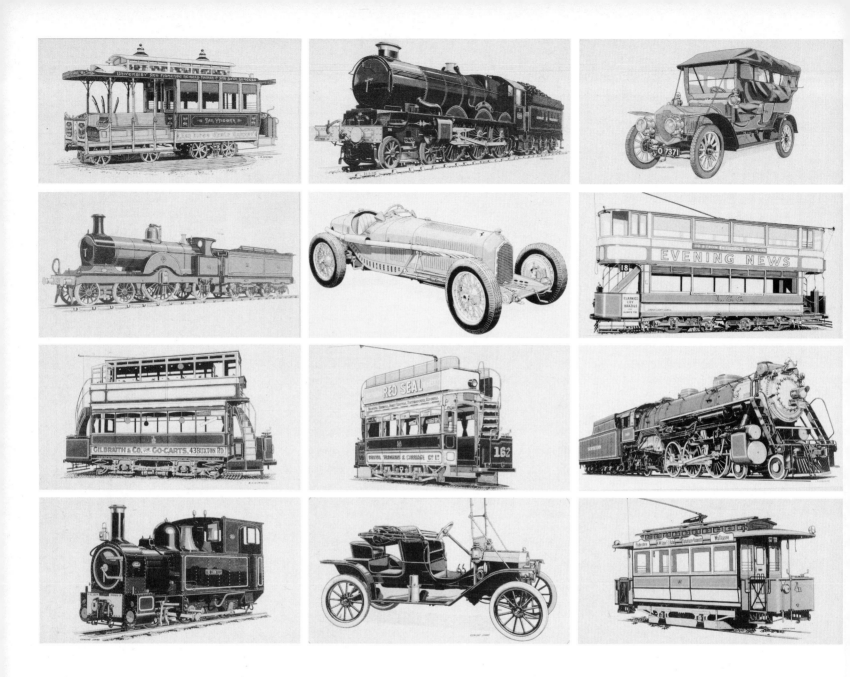

Here is another Premium Show discovery. Original lithographs and collector reproductions produced by Prescott-Pickup Co., Ltd. and handled in the U.S. by Robert Durr Enterprises, Ltd., P.O. Box 343, Morris Plains, NJ 07950. These unique lithos cover the full gamut of subject material from Steam Locomotives, Trolley cars, Vintage automobiles and Buses, all the way to Ships, Aircraft and Military Uniforms.

They will add a nice touch to many of your displays and promotions. Write to Robert Durr Enterprises for complete details.

A most unusual material is available from Ray Draper Associates, 330 Edgewood Ave., Westfield, NJ 07090. Quick projects are possible with fast working SCULPTURFOAM. The high density mass is an excellent sculpturing medium for displayers and artists. Available in blocks of various sizes, SCULPTURFOAM can be easily shaped with a knife or saw. Hand or power sanding produces smooth marble-like qualities or rough-hewn granite textures. Strong and lightweight, an eight-foot statue weighs about 35 pounds. SCULPTURFOAM can be painted, stained or metallized for various surface effects. This new art medium is just the ticket for sculptors who have always wanted to do a large piece but could never afford genuine marble. Additionally, SCULPTURFOAM is light enough so that the floor does not need additional support.

Lord Nelson would have loved Bellerophon books!

These unique Coloring Books each have fifty pages printed on good sturdy paper and we think that they are some of the greatest guides for reference that we have ever seen. This montage of covers gives you an idea of the wide variety of subjects and titles available and on the next three pages we have received permission to reproduce 16 line drawings from some of the books. Please understand that all illustrations are copyrighted by Bellerophon books and should not be reproduced. They are available at most book stores or write to — Bellerophon Books, 153 Steuart St., San Francisco, Calif. 94105.

Mother Goose

Shakespeare

Ancient Egypt

Ancient Near East

Chaucer

Ancient Egypt

PAGE 374/SUPPLIERS

Japan

Incas, Aztecs & Mayas

Ships

American Indians

Renaissance

Henry VIII and his Wives

Japan

Queen Elizabeth

American Revolution

Middle Ages

Livingstone Evans Enterprises, 916 North LaCienega Blvd., Los Angeles, Calif. 90069 has a very unique line of Americana archive engravings covering many subjects, plus a line of dimensional letters called "Alphabets in Dimension" They specialize in designing and manufacturing wall decor and decorative accessories. To obtain a copy of their latest catalog, write on your business letterhead.

Gargoyles Ltd., 512 South Third Street, Society Hill, Phila., Penna. 19147 was mentioned in our Almanac Section and in the Londonderry Section.

This is a very exciting and unique firm, whose business is "living in the past" and to quote their brochure "They offer a most distinguished collection of the architectural heritage of Europe and America". Here is a partial list of their offerings. Terra Cotta Cherubs, side boards, waitress stations and display counters, brass and iron brackets and gates, beveled crystal doors imported from Belgium, old fashioned ceiling fans, the Nations most complete selection of authentic antique shop fronts, rail and nautical memorabilia, Victorian wash basins and pedestals and cast iron spiral stair cases from Great Britain and Spain.

Your personal copy of their most unusual catalog is available at $4.00.

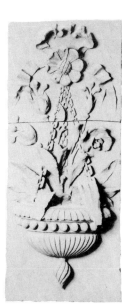

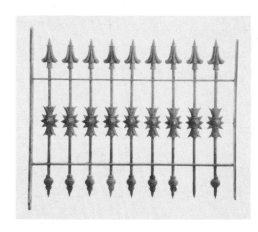

Spanjer Brothers, Inc., 1160 North Howe Street, Chicago, Ill. 60610, has been a major supplier of sign letters and decor for over three quarters of a Century. They have expanded their retail decor program to include: Griffins, Fingers, Suns, Fascia Panels, Fragments and Heraldic Devices. In addition to this grouping they now offer the EGS/500 INTERIOR Graphic Signing Program. This consists of 5 basic units, which are completely modular. Each unit accommodates changeable copy inserts. Write for complete details on all programs to Spanjer, mentioning The Designer's Dictionary.

Alexander H. Girard

*EGS/500 is a trademark of Environmental Graphic Systems, Inc., Chicago

Herman Miller commissioned Alexander Girard to design a group of fabric panels, whose functions are the screening of space and the absorption of sound. We were so impressed with the design quality that we readily recommend them as display units for all kinds of backdrops and hangings. Think how impressive the double heart panel on page 384 in hot pink and red would be as a backdrop for a Valentine's Day promotion, and the jar of pebbles next to it for a Penny Candy Idea. Herman Miller Showrooms are located in Chicago, Los Angeles, Madison Avenue and Washington, D.C.

Write to Herman Miller, Inc., Zeeland, Michigan 49464, for brochure and showroom addresses.

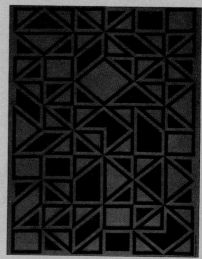

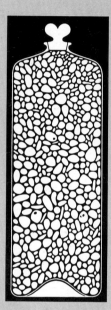

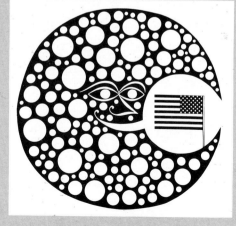
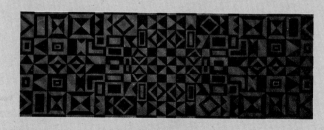

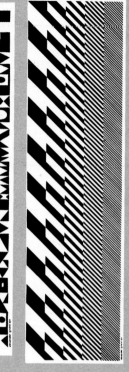

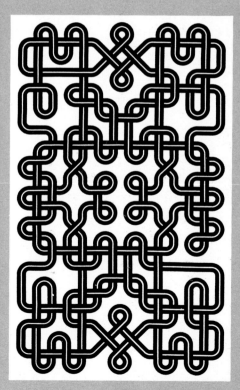

KIDSWORLD

orient express

Hoe Hoe Hoe

DECORATIVE

WESTERN STORE

Penny Candy

Ski-daddle

THE POTTING SHED

Gingerbread

FROMAGE

RUSSIAN EASTER

LONDONDERRY

Shellgame

Giants

BI-CENTENNIAL

Summer Stuff

Banners

ATRIUM

FUN

CHEESE?

Photo Lettering Incorporated, 216 East 45th Street, New York 10017, has been our source for many of the unusual headings used in some of our sections. They are one of the countries largest producers of Photo Lettering, offering literally hundreds of styles, plus a full selection of Border, Cosmographs and Special Effects. They also offer a service called, "Spectrakrome". This is a special "color magic" process that takes a black and white mechanical and converts it into a color matched preview print in a variety of colors. With this method you can see the finished package, ad, etc., before printing. Write for details on their lettering style offerings and other services.

International Design Corporation, 1147 West Ohio St., Chicago, Ill. 60622, presents these unusual display units entitled, "Corrugated Buildups". These displayers have been made entirely of corrugated board and have a "natural" look to them. These, along with other unique display units, are available from International Design.

Austen Display Corporation, 133 W. 19th Street, New York 10011, offers a huge line of graphics. We think they are terrific for window backdrops, to wrap around columns and to hang from the ceiling, not only as a central design theme, but also to fill large voids, where other display materials will not work. These prints are available in black/white, sepia/beige and prints on fabric (available only in black and white). Prints can be custom colored at additional cost and all prints are delivered on 42″ wide material in lengths up to 96″ high. The categories are: Animals, Antiques, Architecture, Back to School, Back to College, Cars, Christmas, Easter, Far East, Flowers, Fruits, Vegetables, Heads, Figures, Illustrations, Graphic Art, Kitchen Utensils, Food, Housewares, Landmarks, Monuments, Landscapes, Mother's Day, Father's Day, Movie Stars, Music Instruments, Plants, Leaves, Soldiers, Sports, Suns, Rain, Textures, Patterns, Surfaces, Trees, Typography, Lettering, Signs, Valentine.

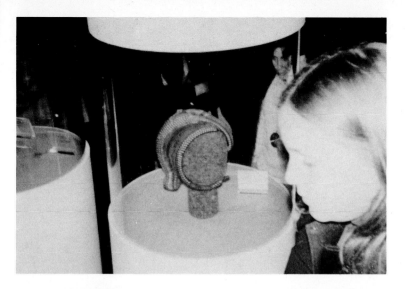

Project Seven, 1064 River Road, Edgewater, NJ 07020. This firm has developed a new product in cooperation with Sonoco products. It is Concavex, a semi-round, self supporting, rigid paper laminate. They can be used for arches, backgrounds, column covers, partitions, light troughs and reflectors and for store fixtures.

Other full rounds are available for exhibits and displays. Finishes include aluminum, silver foil, cork, burlap, etc.

Write Marvin Eppy, President.

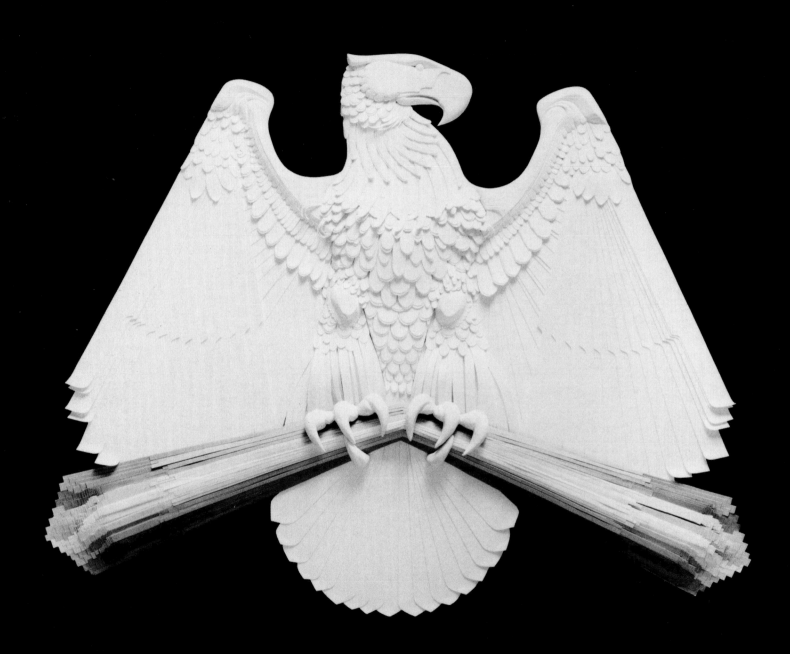

We are indebted to the Simpson Lee Paper Company for loaning us this picture of this beautiful paper-sculpture eagle. It's richly detailed and might be a display idea for your Bi-Centennial promotion.

In every Upson promotion we have mentioned the use of felt in one way or another and this book would not be complete without giving you a little black and white preview of Allied Felt's new promotional offering entitled, "The Rise & Felt of the Western World". It is a charming full color set of illustrations designed by Ray Ameijide. He is one of New York's outstanding illustrators and has recently received the Top Award for "Illustrator of the Year" by virtue of his felt sculptures, not only for the aforementioned promotion, but for other advertising clients. The illustration shown on this page is the introductory design and the 8 illustrations shown on pages 392 and 393 will give you an idea of how clever this talented man is and how beautifully felt handles, not only for art work of this kind, but for all kinds of display work. Allied Felt (New York office, 24 W. 25th St., New York — Shipping Center, 46 Star Lake Ave., Bloomingdale, NJ 07403) offers 36 different colors of felt by the yard in two qualities. Fashion felt (12 oz.) and Kraft felt (9 oz.). They also offer felt squares and assorted craft kits. Send for their current swatch book.

Scandanavia has always been in the forefront of excellent design, craftsmanship and tradition. Our section on this theme takes many directions. As we have described in the other sections of the book, one of these elements can be used or the entire theme can be used for a store-wide promotion. Naturally, we have shown lots of good strong Viking figures, banner designs and other display elements, to help you formulate your program.

We start with this multi-screen design for a shop that could be called, "The Land of the Midnite Sun" or merely, "Midnite Sun". We have tried to capture the feeling of the north. The Viking figure in the foreground could be cut from ¼″ Upson; a dimensional effect is achieved with small wooden blocks between the two panels and the edge treated with ⅛″ Upson easy curve. The color scheme could be a space blue and sun yellow, from the House and Garden group.

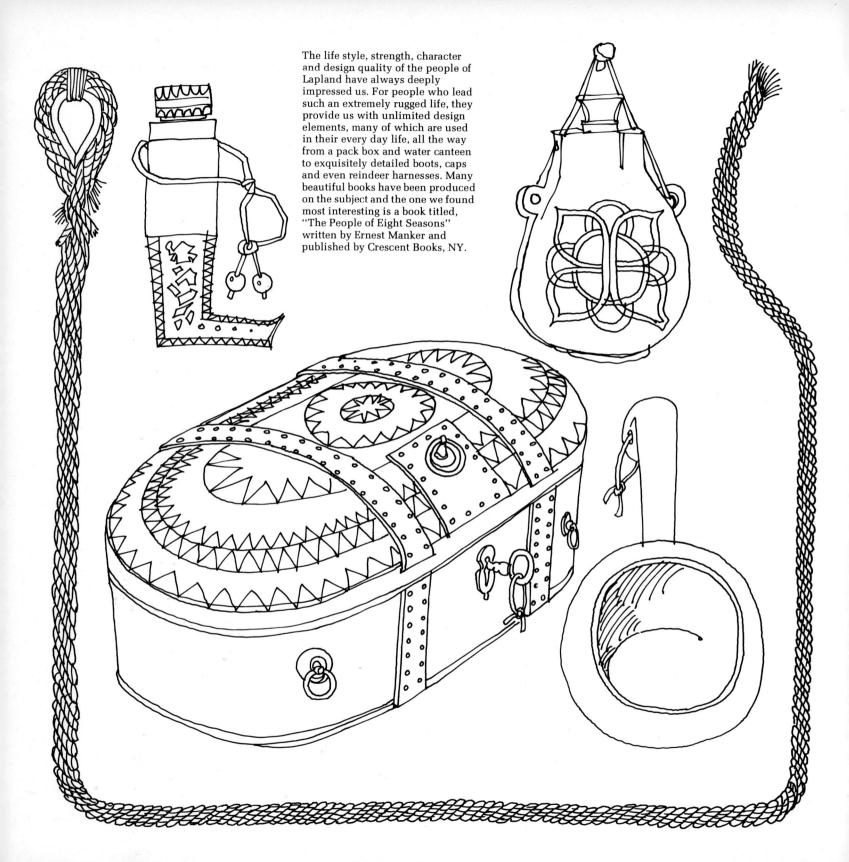

The life style, strength, character and design quality of the people of Lapland have always deeply impressed us. For people who lead such an extremely rugged life, they provide us with unlimited design elements, many of which are used in their every day life, all the way from a pack box and water canteen to exquisitely detailed boots, caps and even reindeer harnesses. Many beautiful books have been produced on the subject and the one we found most interesting is a book titled, "The People of Eight Seasons" written by Ernest Manker and published by Crescent Books, NY.

A store wide promotion will be enhanced with a fanciful architectural facade idea to be used either outside or inside the store. By designing the exterior facade around your existing windows it is possible to achieve a true Scandanavian street scene, using Upson ⅜″ All Weather Panels with stained boards for beamed effects and subtle stucco textures on other building walls.

By carrying this idea inside the store these same backgrounds can be used along one large wall or actually formed into a street of shops.

The pole and panel idea can be used effectively as a space divider or as a background idea for windows.

Throughout Scandinavia one finds hundreds of colorful banners and unique signs of all kinds. Vikingsholm can be the name of your import shop and the gigantic banner with the Viking figures could hang outside, announcing your Scandia promotion.

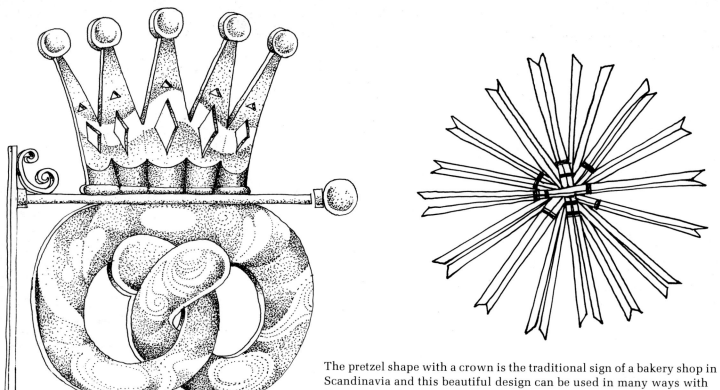

The pretzel shape with a crown is the traditional sign of a bakery shop in Scandinavia and this beautiful design can be used in many ways with Upson. It can be sprayed gold or produced completely in three dimensional form.

Christmas and straw from golden wheat are synonymous and this example of Danish Folk Art could be used throughout the store.

BLOMMOR

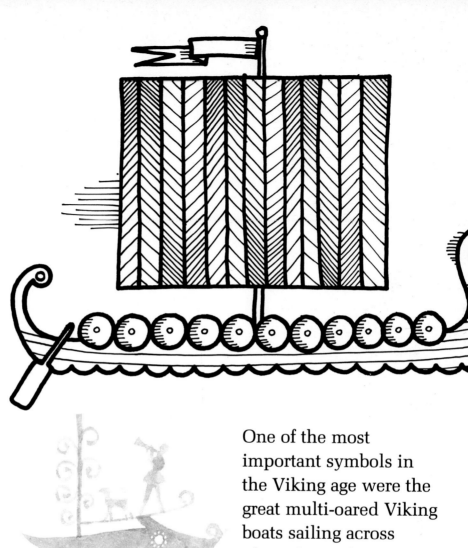

One of the most important symbols in the Viking age were the great multi-oared Viking boats sailing across The Atlantic from 800 to 1050 A.D.

We have shown this symbol as a central form for your promotion, along with a felt banner incorporating the famous drinking toast, "SKAL".

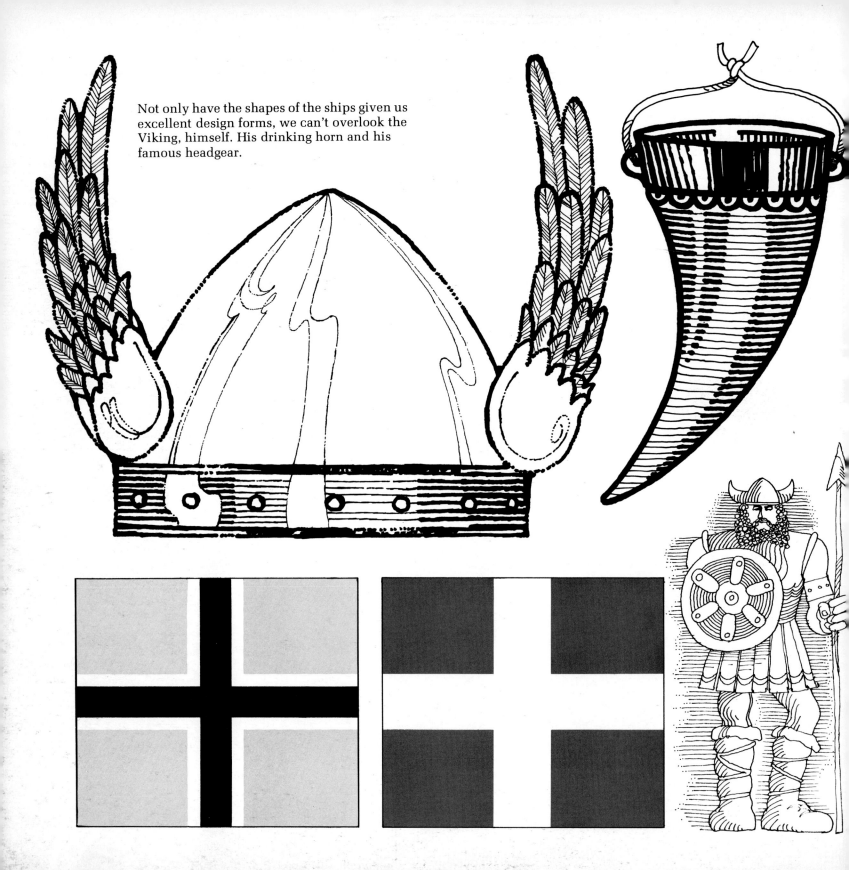

Not only have the shapes of the ships given us excellent design forms, we can't overlook the Viking, himself. His drinking horn and his famous headgear.

WESTERN STORE
WESTERN STORE

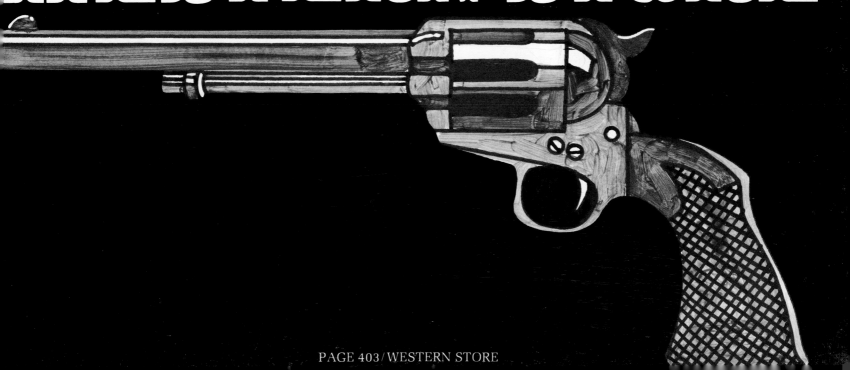

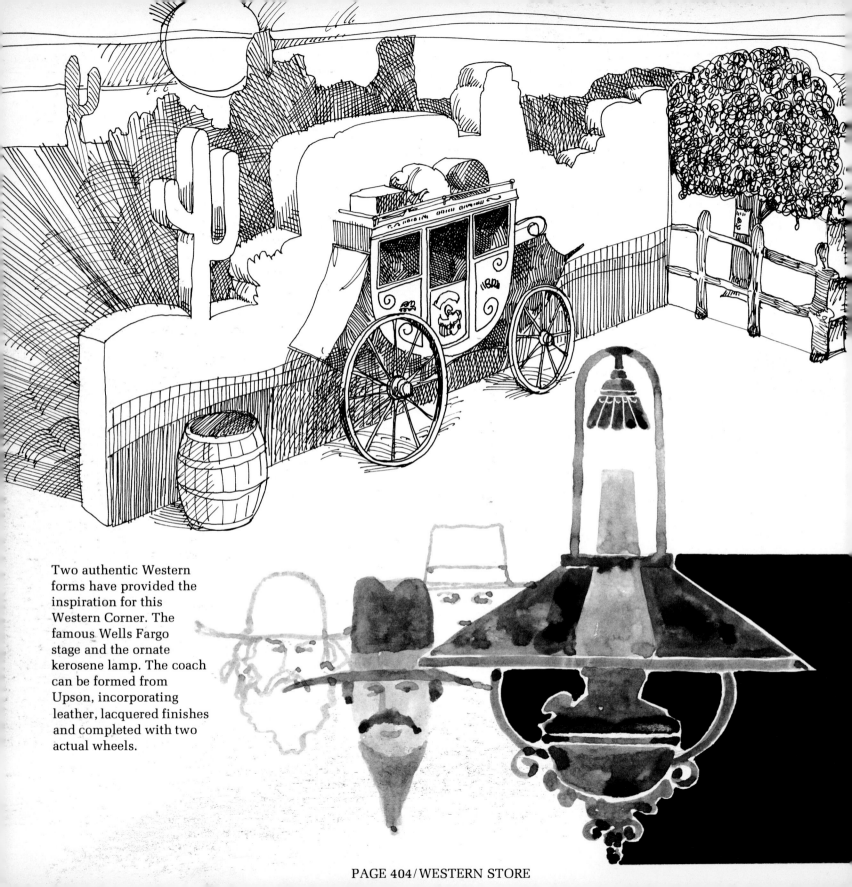

Two authentic Western forms have provided the inspiration for this Western Corner. The famous Wells Fargo stage and the ornate kerosene lamp. The coach can be formed from Upson, incorporating leather, lacquered finishes and completed with two actual wheels.

This handsome window background was inspired by the famous Durham smoking tobacco pouch. This form could be produced by making the basic shape out of Upson, stapling some type of soft stuffing to the outside and covering it all with linen or canvas.

NET WEIGHT
5/8
OUNCE

GENUINE
DURHAM
(TRADE MARK)

Smoking Tobacco

W.T. BLACKWELL & CO.,
(BLACKWELL'S DURHAM TOB. CO., Suc'r.)

THE AMERICAN TOBACCO CO., SUCCESSOR.
RICHMOND, VIRGINIA

NONE GENUINE WITHOUT THE BULL ON EACH PACKAGE

THE TEN GALLON WESTERN STORE

This photograph came from one of our past promotions and it is so richly detailed that we wanted to reproduce it again for you. It can be handled in many ways, both as a Western back-wall or an actual entrance for your store or boutique.

Index

Notes

Notes

Notes

Notes

Notes

Notes